THE HEART OF AN ADOPTIVE MOM

ADOPTION
#NotPlanB

A Companion for First Time Adoptions

Kelley Lambert

THE HEART OF AN ADOPTIVE MOM

A Companion for First Time Adoptions

Kelley Lambert

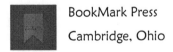

BookMark Press
Cambridge, Ohio

Unless otherwise indicated, Scripture quotations are from the New International Version (NIV)

Holy Bible, New International Version®, NIV® Copyright ©1973, 1978, 1984, 2011 by Biblica, Inc.® Used by permission. All rights reserved worldwide.

THE HEART OF AN ADOPTIVE MOM: A Companion for First Time Adoptions

Authored by Kelley Lambert

ISBN-13: **978-1720799559**

ISBN-10: **1720799555**

FORWARD

Why I wrote this book.

During our adoption, I kept searching for the adoption book. You know, the one that had all the answers. The one that would tell me exactly what to expect. Yeah. That never happened. Or, at least not for me. I found tons of books for adoptive families and books on how to adjust to coming home, but none were written for me, the (adoptive) (1st time) momma. For some reason, "The top ten things I wish I would have known when I was adopting" was never a list that spread like wildfire on Facebook. Man, wouldn't that have been great.

This book. It's for you, mom. Are you thinking about adoption, but have heard it's too hard? Too big? Takes too long? Costs too much? You're too old? It's just not doable? Well, can I take just one minute to encourage you? God is the author of adoption in that we are made in the image of God and God is love. He created it the moment he created us in His image. It's His idea that we love others. With Him, it's not too hard, it doesn't take too long, it doesn't cost too much, and you're never too old. It's totally doable. If you're on a time crunch, go ahead and jump to "Spoonful of Sugar." I saved this chapter for the end because it has a lot of spoilers in our story. But if you're debating whether or not adoption is right for you, it's a perfect place to start.

Otherwise, here I am, at 1:13 in the morning, typing when I should be sleeping. Because we all know the rule: *sleep when the baby sleeps.* Rebel. Oh yeah. Don't get me wrong; I really want to sleep. Like, really really. But, there's so much I want to say to you. So much I want you to know. I want to sit down with every (adoptive) momma, have a nice cup of coffee, and tell you, with love and tenderness, what these next few years are going to hold. Did you catch that? Years. So, since it might be a while before we meet, and you've got a long road ahead, and I've got a bottle to warm for the next feeding, let's get started.

DEDICATION

Because I couldn't have done it without you.

This book, for sure, is about adoption. There's no denying that. But to me, this is a book truly about God's goodness. And nothing else. In our story, you'll see over and over again how God used people to do BIG things in our adoption. How He showed His goodness through the community around us.

With that said, there are a few people I want to thank for offering themselves up as vessels of God's goodness to be poured out on our family.

- My mom. Do you remember the day in your office when you told one of your doctors that we were going to adopt, and with a smile on your face, you said, "I knew she was going to do something like that"? I'll never be able to explain the significance of those words to me. With that one sentence, you- the most important person in my life (aside from Chase, of course)- affirmed God's calling on my life. You didn't question it. You affirmed it. And, you were proud. Mom, no matter how far apart we've lived, you were always the first call I made, for good news and bad. You were there. I trusted your wisdom and relished your comfort. You were the biggest reminder of the promises of God because, with each word, each phone call, each hug, each tear, I felt the love of God. Mom, I love you. I'm so glad our children call you "Gran."

- Our families. You have loved so sacrificially. You give and give and give. You jumped on board with our adoption day 1. You've spent hours on the road and hours in the air to share the love of God with our children. Thank you. Thank you for never letting us be too far away to feel your love.

• Our church in NC. You guys. Do you have any idea how much we love you? Well, we love you so stinkin' much. Y'all remember the first time we had small-group in our house after our son came home? How crazy cool was that to have him in the very same house we'd been praying for him to come home to for over 3 years? There's no way for me to truly say thank you for everything you did for us and the thousands of ways you served our families. You just mean so much to us. From the yard sales to the gala, to the t-shirts, to the airport, you showed up. You guys were always there. Thank you. Thank you. Thank you. There won't be a time when we look back on our adoption and don't think of you.

• My work family. From Cook and UCES. Y'all were my family away from home. From Friday afternoons at First Street to late afternoon's in Carrie's classroom, you were my family. You were there when I got the Thursday updates. You took care of everything when I was in Africa. And you simply adored my son. You could have easily counted it a loss to have someone join your staff, your team, that would soon be out on FMLA, but yet, you counted it a joy. So, from the bottom of my heart, I love you. Thank you. I hope, one day soon, we'll all be together again.

• To the one who gave us the $1,400.00 I want you to know that when I think of you, my heart swells with gratitude. You were the "go button" on our adoption. When I see our son ride his bike without training wheels, I am so stinkin' thankful you gave.

He came home! Thank you. May the Lord bless you with how richly you blessed us.

• To my person. My bestie. My BFF. Thank you. This book would probably still be 18,000 words without you. I never want to do life without you. If God willed it, I'd hop on a plane and move in with you asap. We'd be the coolest moms ever, and our kids would grow up together. But since that's not in the plans for today, know that every day, I think of you, and I'm proud to call you *friend*. God is doing a mighty work in your life, and He is using you to show other mommas how to live in obedience to the Gospel as a wife and a mom. You are important. You are special. You're one of a kind. If you write a book, I'll be first to buy it.

To my husband. Thanks for being the calm in the storm. For doing the things, I didn't want to do. For not losing your cool when I blew gaskets. For being a loving husband and father who leads his family in obedience to the Gospel and submission to the authority of the Lord our God. I don't just like you. I love you like a rock.

•

Table of Contents

Adoption and Orphan Care

James 1:27 Updated American standard Version (UASV)

[27] Pure and undefiled religion before our God and Father is this: to visit orphans and widows in their affliction, and to keep oneself unstained by the world.

SO, YOU CAN'T GET PREGNANT

Because clearly, that's the only reason people adopt.

One of my favorite memories of our adoption story was from a conversation I had with a coworker. It was the beginning of the school year and my first-year teaching at this particular school. The PTA was throwing us a luncheon as we geared up for another year of teaching. In the midst of talk of lesson plans, rosters, and first-day activities, one teacher leaned across the table and asked, "So, why are you adopting?" Naturally, I explained that the Bible calls us very clearly to "look after orphans and widows in their distress," James 1:27[1]. "So, that's what we're doing. We're Christians. We believe what the Bible says. So, that's what we're doing," I said.

After a moment, she leaned forward. Then whispered, "So that's, (long pause), the *only* reason you're adopting." Immediately, I knew what she was asking. However, I didn't want to answer *that* question. I wanted my response that Jesus said to adopt was a good enough reason to adopt, to be enough. It was for me. It should be for her, too. Or at least, that's what I thought. So, instead, I responded, "We haven't tried to get pregnant if that's what you're asking."

And with that, the wind out of our adoption sails stopped flapping. Doesn't that suck? Here I am, doing this pretty awesome thing. This thing that God thinks pretty highly of. I mean. Hello. He adopted us. He told us to

---

[1] *Holy Bible*, New International Version. Grand Rapids: Zondervan House, 2002. Print

adopt. Seems like a good enough reason to be obedient. Adoption is awesome. Who needs to ask questions?

Well. Yeah. Everybody does. And everybody will. Get ready. Dear sister, I want you to know with conviction that adoption is beautiful and holy. And the only reason *you* need to adopt is that God adopted us. However, *they* will need more. And, you will need *them.*

During our fundraising process, I approached a friend who had pretty top connections in the city and asked her help to spread the word for our adoption gala. I was hoping she'd help us sell 50-100 tickets, or at least get donors. Something. Anything. Instead, what I got was an email a few days later, "Kelley, I really don't understand why you expect other people to fund your adoption. This is a very private thing and an expense that most people should and do incur on their own." Yeah. She assumed we were adopting because we couldn't get pregnant and thought it was socially inappropriate to ask other people to give us money to adopt.

Plan B. That's what they're going to assume your adoption is. Because why would anyone want to go through this process voluntarily? It's like $30,000. Tons of time. Tons of money. Butt loads of paperwork. Why would anyone do that willingly?

Sister, those are the questions you gotta be prepared to answer. Why? Because at the root of all of those questions, is the Gospel. It's the opportunity to share your story. Your child's story. It's the opportunity to talk about Jesus. It's the most important thing. He's the most important thing.

No matter how you came into this journey, whether through infertility, divine intervention, or pure obedience, adoption is your story. And, it's their story too, if they'll believe.

So, when we were asked those questions, we took every opportunity to point our story back to Jesus. After all, He's the author of it.

Romans 8:15-17: *So, you have not received a spirit that makes you fearful slaves. Instead, you received God's Spirit when he adopted you as his own children. [h] Now we call him, "Abba, Father." [i] For his Spirit joins with our spirit to affirm that we are God's children. And since we are his children, we are his heirs. In fact, together with Christ we are heirs of God's glory.*

Our first response was always that we adopt because we were adopted. Through no righteousness of our own, we became heirs of God's glory. It was not because of work or deed that we earned that love. It was given to us. That's why we adopt. That's why we love.

We love because He first loved us. 1 John 4:19

That's all you need. That's reason enough. Please hear me loud and clear mommas, whether you are adopting because you felt an initial pull to adopt regardless of fertility status, or because of infertility, it doesn't matter. We adopt because He adopted us. That's what it comes down to. We love, because He first loved us. But still, the Gospel gives us way more reason to adopt:

Religion that God our Father accepts as pure and faultless is this: to look after orphans and widows in their distress.– James 1:27

Speak up for those who cannot speak up for themselves; ensure justice for those being crushed. Yes, speak up for the poor and helpless and see that they get justice. – Proverbs 31:8-9

You are the helper of the fatherless. Lord, You have heard the desire of the humble; You will prepare their heart; You will cause Your ear to hear, to do justice to the fatherless and the oppressed, That the man of the earth may oppress no more. – Psalms 10:14,17-18

Anyone who welcomes a little child like this on my behalf is welcoming me. – Matthew 18:5

And, you know what's crazy? Even after you quote scripture and sit down in coffee houses with friends, they're still going to wonder. They're still going to expect. They're going to assume, you just can't get pregnant. Even if you are great people with big hearts who love God. That's likely to not be enough, still.

So, I wrote a blog. After all, a majority of our networking was done on social media. So, this is what I wrote- And momma's, if infertility jump-started your adoption, this could be a good conversation starter for you, too:

So, you can't get pregnant?

This is usually the response we get when someone learns we're adopting. Understandable, of course. **However, us being able or not able to get pregnant has nothing to do with why we're adopting.** *In fact, we haven't even tried to get pregnant. Why not? Because it's not enough to know the statistics listed below... we need to do something about them.*

Here Is Why

- There are 4.3 million orphans in Ethiopia alone. One in six of them will die before their 5th birthday. One. In. Six. That is a crazy ridiculous number that could be lower. So much lower. If all we did was give them food.
- Every day: 5,760 more children become orphans.
- Every Year in Africa Alone: 2,102,400 more children become orphans

- 143,000,000: The number of orphans who spend an average of 10 years in an orphanage or foster home.
- 153,000,000: The number of orphans worldwide.

Why Adopt? There are 153 million children who DON'T HAVE HOMES. Chase and I. Well, we have a home, with some empty bedrooms. And, we have a refrigerator, with some food.

James 1:27- Pure and genuine religion is this: to take care of orphans and widows.

It's time church. Let's step up. Let's bring these children home. It's time to LOVE BIG.

Advances in Public Health. Volume 2017, Article ID 7479295, 10 pages[2]

SOS Children's Villages - USA, Inc.[3]

Skyward Journey. Life. Adoption. Discovery:[4]

You would not believe the number of shares and requests to share this blog I received. I had numerous people address me in person and tell me how powerful those words were to them. Even months into the process, I had people ask me to repost this very blog.

Know the heart of why you're adopting - because of God. Then, be prepared to stand for the vulnerable. A huge part of taking care of orphans is advocating for them. Everyone will not adopt. That's just a fact. But, when you start making people aware of what's really going on in the world, what's going on outside of their local news channel, eyes are opened, and hearts are softened. So even if they

[2] https://doi.org/10.1155/2017/7479295
[3] https://www.sos-usa.org/our-impact/childrens-statistics
[4] https://skywardjourney.wordpress.com/orphan-statistics/

may not decide to adopt themselves, they might just decide to partner with you and bring your children home.

Again, let me speak to the hearts of you precious mommas whose hearts are stronger than most: to those mommas who are battling infertility. You are choosing to adopt. You didn't give up. You could have. You could have accepted your infertility and moved on. But you are choosing to press on and run this race of adoption. That is HUGE mommas. Do not let anyone steal your joy of adoption or count it any less that infertility is what prompted your adoption. You are making a choice. A choice to adopt. A choice to be obedient to God's calling to take care of vulnerable children. And that is what matters!

But I can almost guarantee, if you don't start telling your story, no one else will share it for you, and no one will get involved. People will take their lead from you. People will decide if adoption is good or bad based on your experience. They'll decide if governments are corrupt based on what you say. They'll decide if adoption is only negative or if it turns their hearts back to Jesus, based on your story. So, know why you do what you do. And then, tell others about it.

If you need one more reminder- We adopt, because He adopted us.

And, can I put one more thought out there, one more sentiment? One more truth? This is Plan A for your life. Whether you have come into adoption because of a stirring in your heart or through a road of infertility, this is God's Plan A for you. For your children. He knew, before your time on this earth began, the children that you would shepherd and disciple. He knew the names of your children. He knew how they would come into your life. **So, while perhaps maybe your journey to adoption didn't come about in a way you would have imagined, it's exactly what God has called us to.** Welcome to Plan A.

I'M NOT JEALOUS THAT YOU'RE PREGNANT

At least that's what I kept telling myself.

At one point during our three years, I literally told Chase, my husband, "This is fair warning that you better buy some happy sleeves because this momma can't wait any longer." Oh, I struggled. And even as we're home with our son now, I still struggle. In fact, a large reason we went with our adoption agency over another was that the other one told us that if we were to get pregnant during the process that the adoption would be put completely on hold and that all paperwork would need to be redone. Yeah, no thanks.

Even though we went with an agency that was compassionate and understanding with families who conceived throughout the adoption process, we had a hard time reconciling getting pregnant and adopting at the same time. But, oh boy, did we want to.

For us, it just didn't make sense. At the time, we requested 2 children. Meaning, if we were to get pregnant, we'd automatically become a family of 5. Now, while people do it all the time who have triplets, I just didn't see that working for us. It wasn't practical. (Honestly, I couldn't figure out the room and board situation. I mean, where's my mom gonna stay when she comes to help out with the babies, if there's so many babies that they've taken over the guest room? First world problems, I know!)

Also, financially it would have made things very difficult. How could we have explained that- yes, we need your money for our adoption, but we can handle the one in my belly? It just didn't sit right with us. It would have also been tough to pay for the hospital stay and a trip to Africa at the same time. Let alone, being stressed about timing. What if we got the call to go to Ethiopia while I was 8 or 9 months pregnant and couldn't travel? Or what if we did travel and I got sick on the plane? (Oh wait, that did happen, and I wasn't pregnant. So, good luck with that one, peeps.) I literally- secretly- stressed about this the whole time. Even though we were on birth control, and had been for years, I was afraid I'd have super eggs that'd be like Mrs. Pacman. They'd just gobble up all of his sperm and I'd be mom to quintuplets. No matter that the birth control we'd used since getting married had never failed us, I was terrified of getting pregnant. Needless to say, we wasted a lot of money on pregnancy tests. PSA- The Dollar Tree sales them for $1, but you've got to ask. They make it super comfortable for you, by making you ask for them for one, since they're kept behind the counter. Apparently, they're a hot commodity. Who knew?

There were other things to consider too, that you should as well. FMLA. You only get 12 weeks in a calendar year. So, if you take 12 weeks starting in April, your time wouldn't refresh again until the next July. Yeah. Timing is super important.

Even with all of the information. All of the reasons it would have made no sense to get pregnant, it hurt so much when someone got pregnant. You know. Those cute little pictures people post on Facebook to announce that they're pregnant. The ones with the 3 pairs of shoes: daddy's shoes, mommy's shoes, and baby's shoes. Breaks your heart. Every single time. Or the announcements that tell you whether they're having a boy or a girl. That's pretty tough. Especially when you're waiting for an email to tell you the same information they'll get by slicing into a cake or opening a box with pink balloons floating out. Or, how about walking past a maternity store and doing everything you can to not shrivel up with so much envy that those mothers get a big ole' belly to tell the world they've got a bundle of joy on the way. What do you get? A pile of paperwork.

And you know what, it goes beyond just the announcements. It's the updates. The ones where moms post the "one month" picture with the little card on the baby's belly that tells you how old they are, next to a chalkboard that's very cutely decorated with all sorts of fun facts about him/her. And all you want to do is scream about how unfair it is! It's so freakin' unfair that they get all of those moments and you get none. You have no idea what your child likes to eat, likes to do. You didn't get to hear their first words or watch their first steps. You weren't there to take a one month, two month, or 1-year photo. There was no birthday party. You. Weren't. There.

Oh, and can we talk about breastfeeding? How your child (possibly) won't be breastfed? I didn't even know I wanted to breastfeed until I realized it wasn't even an option. Then, I began forward thinking and started trying to decide, can I even breastfeed children I have biologically-If I can have them? Will that cause hurt to my adopted children to realize that I wasn't able to breastfeed them because they weren't "mine." Oh, that awful word.

Is that real enough for you? That's what to expect mom. That's why I want you to hear me loud and clear about this pregnancy thing. Make up your mind now. Know definitively what your stance on pregnancy is. Because it is going to be tough. Have friends that will stand by you and stand firm. Friends that will remind you of the calling on your life to adopt. I'll talk more about the importance of your community later. But hear this now, you need them.

For most of our adoption, only my husband knew just how much I was struggling with all of this. Wanting to get pregnant. Wanting to have all of those moments. Knowing it wasn't the time. Knowing through and through that for now, we were called to adopt. Oh, the battle.

Then one night, I lost it. Completely, lost it. My husband and I host a small group. It's a group that meets weekly at our house to discuss the sermon from Sunday and how it applies to our lives. After the sermon recap, we break-off into guys and girls. And on this particular night, I blew a gasket. I started by being the *good* Pastor's Wife by simply saying, "I need y'all to pray for me. I'm struggling right now with wanting to get pregnant, but I know that's not what God has called us to right now." Then, since no one said anything, I just kept going.

... and honestly, I know this makes me awful, but I'm struggling with jealousy too. I want so badly to be pregnant. Every time I see someone who is pregnant, I get so upset. I can't figure out why they get to be pregnant and all I get to do is wait. Someone told me this week, "You need to wait till you get this child home before you start trying." I mean, how ridiculous is that? It's none of her business and she's telling me I shouldn't be trying. No one knows. All of these moms posting pictures and updates of their kids all of the time on Facebook and I'm here like, does anyone care about my kid? Was anyone there for my kid when he was born? No one's there for him. No one. No pictures. No updates. No birthday parties. Stop taking it for granted....

And I just went on and on. It was probably much worse and much longer than I'm remembering. I'm pretty sure no one else got a chance to share that night because I took up so much time. I was simply losing control. I needed to be reminded of what I was called to do. And that's exactly what they did. They prayed over me. And then prayed some more. They followed up with me. They let me know that everything I was feeling was reasonable and that if they were in my shoes, they'd probably feel the same way. To the women who were there in that room with me that night, from the bottom of my heart, thank you. I'll never forget your kindness or the way you gently pointed my heart back to Jesus.

I just needed to be reminded that just because I was called to adopt, didn't mean I wasn't worthy of all of the things a normal mom gets. For some reason, I'd gotten it into my thick noggin that just because I wasn't getting to experience the things that all of the other moms were, that I was less of a mom. Or honestly, that I wasn't even a mom at all.

So, let me set the record straight, now, for you moms going through this very thing. You are a mom. Now. You are the best kind of mom. You love your child before you've ever met them. You've loved them before they were born. You've selflessly given up the right to childbirth. Or, even worse, have had that opportunity and right taken from you, and have chosen to grow them in your heart instead.

You are more mom than some moms will ever be. You've loved your child without circumstance. You're adopting them. You're choosing them. That. Means. Everything. Your life will be spent showing them that they are Plan A. That's a big stinkin' deal.

My best friend told me something once, and I'll never forget it. It was a moment when I was struggling with the possibility of- what if our son hates us and resents us for taking him from his home country? What if he sees us as second best and our love isn't enough? She said, "Then you simply remind him- Son, you were selected, not rejected."

Mommas, guard your heart now. Talk openly with your husband and your adoption agency about pregnancy. You need to know now what will happen if you get pregnant. Even if infertility has been part of your story, it's important to be aware of how a pregnancy can affect an adoption.

Some Questions to Ask

- What is your policy on pregnancy during adoption?
- Will we need to update our home study if we get pregnant?
- What paperwork will need to be updated and what are the related costs?
- Will a pregnancy stop the adoption or delay our referral?

"I DON'T KNOW ABOUT THAT..."

Everyone else's ignorance is not bliss.

My husband and I were at a Christmas party with friends when we shared that we'd received our referral. This was a group of people we'd shared life with for about 3 years at this point. They were friends before adoption was even a topic of conversation for us. So, as you can imagine, we were very excited to share our big news with them. And we weren't just going to shout it out. We decided to do a gender reveal.

Everyone chose a pink or blue heart. They held it up, and we took a picture to remember the sweet moment right before everyone found out if we would be bringing home a little boy or a little girl. Everyone was excited for us and thrilled when we held up our own blue heart. We "oohed" and "awed" over his sweet picture and spent the next several minutes sharing all the wonderful things we already knew about our sweet little man. The night proceeded on, and conversations ebbed and flowed.

Towards the end of the night, we'd separated into men and women while we shared coffee and dessert. The group had relaxed as we'd already been together for several hours. Naturally, people were feeling more and more comfortable with one another. The conversation once again became focused on our adoption.

One of the ladies began wanting to know exactly everything I knew about our son. I shared what I felt like was appropriate without betraying things my son would want held in confidence. After speaking for a few minutes and answering more questions, I made the comment, "Yeah, there are more unknowns in adoptions than in pregnancy." One of the ladies in the group looked at me and said, "I don't know about that." and walked away from all of us.

I went home that evening very perplexed. I couldn't figure out if I'd offended her. Was I wrong? Are there more unknowns in pregnancy than in adoptions? Was it a stupid point to make? Wait, was I even trying to make a point? No, I was just trying to advocate for orphans. No, I didn't do anything wrong.

I really struggled with her reaction to my comment. This lady was among a group of friends we would hang-out with regularly. I didn't want to cause a rift, but I also didn't want to apologize for something that wasn't wrong. So, I sought guidance from my husband and from other moms who'd already bore a biological child. And what it came down to was- no, I wasn't wrong; she simply wasn't educated on adoption.

Here's how we were able to discern the truth in my comment: We compared adoptions vs. pregnancies. Now, granted, there are a thousand circumstances and factors that change with each pregnancy and each adoption. We just made a general list (and our adoptive list was more geared to international adoptions.) It looked something like this:

Pregnancy	Adoption
Birth mom is known.	Birth mom is typically unknown
You are the birth mom, so you know what the	Because the birth mom is unknown or there is no relationship with the birth mom, the adoptive mom

birth mom is putting in her body.	has no knowledge of any drugs or foods that could be ingested and harm the child.
Living conditions of birth mom.	Unknown living conditions of birth mom- Is mom being physically abused which could be harmful to the infant? Does mom have shelter? Food? Water?
Updates of child throughout pregnancy- doctor's appointments, ultrasounds, etc.	No knowledge of child's medical condition while in-utero.
Birth mom is aware of circumstances in which child is being born.	Adoptive parents must trust local/international authorities to ensure that the child is a true orphan and is not being stolen/trafficked.
Guarantee of possession of child- If mom carries to full-term, no one can take the child from her. (Aside from extreme circumstances like DSS).	Throughout any point in an adoption, the adoption can be terminated. Paperwork can be denied. A country can shut down and stop allowing adoptions. A birth mom can change her mind and decide not to proceed with an adoption.

These are just a handful of the factors we looked at to conclude whether or not I was completely off-base. Based on the facts we presented above, I was pretty on-point. Generally speaking, there are more unknowns in adoptions than in pregnancies.

All-in-all, does this really matter? Does it matter if I was right or if I was wrong? Yes and no.

In the big scheme of things, it doesn't really matter. Both pregnancies and adoptions, are pretty stinking hard and have a thousand challenges each unique to themselves. Having now adopted and had a pregnancy, I know those things are true.

But in regard to your adoption, it does matter. A whole heck of a lot. Why? Because the more uneducated people are, the fewer people there are to stand for vulnerable children in this world. And that's super important when we remember that as believers, we are called to take care of orphans. Remember, adoption is not our idea, it's His idea. And if it's His idea, it should be important to us. Additionally, the fewer people are educated on adoption, the fewer people there will be that can support you and your family through this adoption. After all, it's hard to care about something you have no knowledge of.

If we truly believe we are called to take care of orphans (James 1:27), then we must be willing to take charge and break down the barriers that adoptive children and adoptive families are going to face. We must be advocates for them. If not us, then who?

We've got to be willing to have tough conversations. Especially with those, we are close to. If we aren't willing to have a tough conversation with someone we love, how on earth are we going to make it through the adoption process when we've got not just one person who isn't our biggest fan, but a government that seems to be working against us? A government that is in no rush to complete our paperwork? Or, an agent or social worker who, for whatever reason, seems to be anti-adoption and yet we need them to sign-off on our paperwork?

Know, before you get started, the realities of adoption. Know why you're adopting. Then, share those truths.

THE HARDEST PART

When someone else decides whether or not your child comes home.

There were a thousand hard parts to this adoption. A thousand. But the hardest was when we hit paperwork jams. Our adoption went incredibly smoothly the first year and a half. Like crazy smooth. So much so that I was like, "Who are all these crazy people saying adoption is hard?"

Yeah. Everything came to a screeching halt at the beginning of 2015 for us. We got a notice from USCIS that all of our paperwork was expiring in two weeks unless it was updated. I pretty much said, *nuh uh.* The February before, we'd gone to Charlotte to update our fingerprints, since that was the form that was expiring. We knew our prints were expiring, so we went and had them re-done. Piece of cake. Problem solved. Right?

Oh no. Clearly. It wasn't that simple. Even though we went and updated our fingerprints, we didn't actually update our I-171H, which was the form that contained our fingerprint information. Are we serious!?!? How is that even a thing? Even though we sent in the new set of fingerprints on the I-171H form, evidently there was a box on that form that we were supposed to check that would indicate we wanted the form itself to be updated, as well as our fingerprints. Well, we didn't check that box. Had no idea we should even be looking for that box. Had no idea such a box existed.

Here's what this meant for us: If we didn't get that form updated before it expired, our entire adoption would end. We would have to hire a lawyer and make an appeal. At least, that's what we were told. Did we end up running around like a chicken with our heads cut-off? Absolutely! By this point, we already knew who our son was. We'd been receiving weekly updates on him. So, to tell me that if I didn't get a date changed on one seemingly insignificant piece of paper, I'd never get to bring my son home, was absolutely unacceptable. And completely ridiculous.

How is this possible? Please, explain it to me. Help me make sense of it. One piece of paper. One date. Can end it all? In fact, there were several moments like this. Our home study expired because it was such a long process. **(Fun fact- most home studies expire and require updating around 18 months. Some states last a little bit longer. Make sure you know the dates that your home study remains current.)** Then, we had a police officer that was supposed to appear for our first court case just not show up. Not only that, they straight up couldn't find him.

All of these single events were moments in time that- if immediate action was not taken- could have ended our adoption. You'll have these moments, too. Moments where you have to pay hundreds of dollars to change the date on a piece of paper. Moments when you have to live super-lean budget-wise because the adoption agency calls and tells you the fees for paperwork are changing. Moments when things seem so unbelievably unfair. How is it fair that one seemingly small -and maybe even trivial-detail could prevent an orphan from no longer being an orphan, can change everything at the drop of a hat and guarantee that your child is an orphan forever?

Man, that's tough.

Here's my response- How I handled all of these insanely difficult things and crazy moments:

Dear God, please-oh-please, if ever my children are to become among the foster care system or be placed in an orphanage- may the potential adoptive parents be thoroughly investigated and willing to jump-through every crazy hoop and circumstance that is put before them, to ensure that my children are placed with parents that are loving parents that love like you love. Parents that sacrifice for the sake of their children- my children. May they be willing to do whatever it takes to provide for and love my children. Because, Dear Lord, these aren't just my children, they're your children.

Ultimately, isn't that what we'd want? If it was our children being placed in an orphanage? Wouldn't we want their future parents to be as thoroughly vetted as we've been? Why? Because they're worth it. Because we want them to be safe. We want them to be in homes that are going to protect them and love them. If the prospective parents aren't willing to do what we have had to do, would we really want them to be the parents of our children? -- probably not.

So, that's how I rationalize all of the paperwork. All of the hoops. All of the hurdles. All of the frustrations. All of the tears.

Because I'd want someone to be as thoroughly vetted as I've been to gain the honor and privilege of parenting my child.

And in humility, might we offer up that the paperwork and trials we will go through to adopt our child will never compare to the sacrifice of the Cross required for us to become His child.

WHEN THE MAILBOX IS EMPTY

Discouragement and Disappointment

I can't write a book about adoption and not talk about discouragement and disappointment. Whether you're dipping your toes in the waters of adoption or you're underwater, you've already figured out that this beautiful journey is going to be littered with tough times. As much as I'd love to say- I hate that, I can't. Wanna know why? #becauseGod.

Think about the most ultimate level of misery we've ever experienced. That's separation from God.

20 For since the creation of the world God's invisible qualities—his eternal power and divine nature—have been clearly seen, being understood from what has been made, so that people are without excuse. 21 For although they knew God, they neither glorified him as God nor gave thanks to him, but their thinking became futile and their foolish hearts were darkened. (Romans 1:20-21)

There is no greater misery than being cut-off from Christ. But do you know what came out of our greatest despair? Our salvation.

8 But God demonstrates his own love for us in this: While we were still sinners, Christ died for us. (Romans 5:8)

9 If you declare with your mouth, "Jesus is Lord," and believe in your heart that God raised him from the dead, you will be saved. 10 For it is with your heart that you believe and are justified, and it is with your mouth that you profess your faith and are saved. (Romans 10:9-10)

13 for, "Everyone who calls on the name of the Lord will be saved." (Romans 10:13)

So, you see, our worst moment ever, was His greatest moment ever. We were saved.

Mommas, you are going to have so many times when you legitimately feel like you can't go on. It's just too hard. It's just too tough. Even though you know it's worth it. Even though you've already paid thousands of dollars. There will be times when you feel like your next breath may end it all. If you breathe the wrong way things will fall apart. If you have too much hope, you'll overdo it. Or, if you dare doubt that God's going to come through for you, that it won't happen just because you doubted. You will most likely enter this -what feels like- endless cycle of *I'm screwing it all up. It's not going to happen. It's gotta happen. Adoption is His thing. He's going to make it happen. Our forms are expiring. It's not going to happen. It's all my fault. There's no fixing this.*

So, dear momma, may I offer you some hope.

28 Do not be afraid of those who kill the body but cannot kill the soul. Rather, be afraid of the One who can destroy both soul and body in hell. 29 Are not two sparrows sold for a penny? Yet not one of them will fall to the ground outside your Father's care.[b]30 And even the very hairs of your head are all numbered. 31 So don't be afraid; you are worth more than many sparrows. (Matthew 10:28-31)

Oh Mommas. What a good few stinking verses right there! He knows the hairs on your head. Don't be afraid of what's to come. When that paperwork isn't right. When a form is expiring. When you can't get a medical appointment in time. Remember. He's got this. He's got you! He cares so much about you that He knows the number of hairs on your head. Let's take this even one step further. He knows the number of hairs on your child's head. He loves your child, just like He loves you. He's going to take care of you both. And, yes, He even knows how many hairs you lose in the shower each morning. Stop stressing so much.

What about Psalm 139?

16 Your eyes saw my unformed body;

all the days ordained for me were written in your book

before one of them came to be.

17 How precious to me are your thoughts, [a] God!

How vast is the sum of them!

18 Were I to count them,

they would outnumber the grains of sand—

when I awake, I am still with you.

Those were verses I repeated over and over to myself. When I began to struggle with how hard it was to see other mommas get pregnant and wear all the cute maternity clothes- I know what you're thinking- maternity clothes aren't cute. But, you know that old adage- ya always want what ya can't have. I would have to remind myself- the Lord knows my desires. He knows my inmost thoughts. He knows I'm struggling with going months upon months and not hearing anything from our agency. Months of no updates. Months of silence. He knew how much I was hurting. How do I know that? His word says His thoughts about me outnumber the grains of sand. There's so much encouragement in that. When I felt alone- like no one else truly understood how difficult it is to be entire continents away from your child- I relied on this verse. When I felt hopeless because people I'd never met were the ones making life-changing and caregiving decisions about the wellbeing of my child- I had to rely on those verses.

Storytime. So, we got all of our updates a week late. *Quick side-note: Remember in an earlier chapter I talked about struggling with jealousy over other mommas getting to take milestone pictures of their kids? Well, the Lord, He knows our inmost thoughts. After accepting our referral, we began getting weekly updates! Meaning, we would get two pictures of our little man once a week. Isn't He good? He's in the details y'all. Back to the story- The pictures we received each Thursday were actually taken the previous week. This also meant that the health updates we received were already outdated. Once, we received an update that our son had conjunctivitis. Oh, my word y'all. Talk about one freaked out momma. My son. He has conjunctivitis? Okay. What do I do? Wait. I can't do anything. At all. Because, decisions have already been made. This is week-old information. Now, I have to wait until next week to find out if he lost his eyesight. (Yes, my terrified mind went there.) Talk about a tough 7 days. Someone else. Someone I'd never met. Was making decisions for my son's health. How on earth was that happening? How was this acceptable? How could I be sure that he was going to be okay?

Well, I couldn't. There was nothing I could do. So, I prayed. I prayed scripture. I had to remind myself that my son is His son first and foremost. The Lord thought of him in his mother's womb. I didn't begin thinking of adoption until my late teens. But the Lord, well, He had my son in mind long before I ever began caring for him. So, I went to scripture.

25 "Therefore I tell you, do not worry about your life, what you will eat or drink; or about your body, what you will wear. Is not life more than food, and the body more than clothes? *26* Look at the birds of the air; they do not sow or reap or store away in barns, and yet your heavenly Father feeds them. Are you not much more valuable than they? *27* Can any one of you by worrying add a single hour to your life[e]?

28 "And why do you worry about clothes? See how the flowers of the field grow. They do not labor or spin. 29 Yet I tell you that not even Solomon in all his splendor was dressed like one of these. 30 If that is how God clothes the grass of the field, which is here today, and tomorrow is thrown into the fire, will he not much more clothe you— you of little faith? 31 So do not worry, saying, 'What shall we eat?' or 'What shall we drink?' or 'What shall we wear?' 32 For the pagans run after all these things, and your heavenly Father knows that you need them. 33 But seek first his kingdom and his righteousness, and all these things will be given to you as well. 34 Therefore do not worry about tomorrow, for tomorrow will worry about itself. Each day has enough trouble of its own. (Matthew 6:25-34)

So, do this momma. Put your child's name in these verses.

Lord, I will not worry about (your child's name) life. I will not worry about what he will eat or drink, or about his body, or what he will wear. You, Heavenly Father, feed even the birds of the air. My son is much more valuable than them. I cannot add a single hour of worry to my son's life by worrying about him. Lord, I have faith. You know what my son needs. I will seek first your kingdom and your righteousness. I will not worry about tomorrow, for tomorrow will worry about itself.

Now mommas, there's going to be times when you need to pray BIG prayers. Like crazy BIG payers. And, this is an awesome thing. But, to be the one who needs the BIG prayer to be answered, can be pretty scary.

Well, one day in church, I heard a sermon about the Gibeonites battle with the Israelites, their allies, against 5 neighboring kingdoms. Alright, hold the phone. A battle against 5 kingdoms? Are we for real? Is there any way that the Gibeonites come out on top? Well naturally, we are all pretty likely to say *good luck chuck!* Well, in the middle of this battle, Joshua literally commands the sun to stand still. Yes, you read that correctly. He commanded the sun to stand still. Now, Biblically, there's not a whole heap of explanation on why he does this. I'd speculate and say that he wanted more daylight to provide more time for battle, to guarantee the Israelites and Gibeonites victory over the other kingdoms. Any who, he prays that prayer.

Joshua 10:12 *"Sun, stand still over Gibeon, and you, moon, over the Valley of Aijalon."*

Wanna know what happens?

Joshua 10:13 *"So the sun stood still, and the moon stopped, till the nation avenged itself on[5] its enemies, as it is written in the Book of Jashar."*

Joshua prayed that prayer and the Lord gave the Amorites over to the Israelites. Here's another thing I love about this text- ya know- besides the fact that you can pray for the sun to stand still and it will- is the promise held earlier in scripture.

Joshua 10:8 *"The Lord told Joshua, "Don't be afraid of them, for I am handing them over to you. Not one of them can resist you."*

So, here's the rundown:

- Josh (Can I call him that?) is at camp in Gilgal.
- The Gibeonites send word to Josh that they're about to be attacked and could use some help.
- The Lord tells Josh (in nutshell) *Go ahead, I got you.*
- Israelites go and help the Gibeonites fight against the Amorites.
- Josh tells the Sun to stand still.

---

[5] Joshua 10:13 Or *nation triumphed over*

- It does.
- Amorites lose.

Boom. Mind. Blown.

But, did you catch that? The Lord told him to go (pretty much). He said there was no need to be afraid. So, Josh took his troops to battle. Then, having faith in the power and promises of the Lord, Josh told the sun to pause. Like. Literally.

Mommas, I feel like this scripture was put right here for us. Do you realize He's already told you to adopt? He already gave you the "go." It was in James 1:27. You probably know that verse by heart by now. The one with *Take care of orphans and widows.* So, there's nothing to worry about. He told you to do it. So, go do it. He is going to make all the rest fall into line. Don't believe me? Reread those verses earlier from Matthew 6.   He's got this momma. This is HIS thing. Let Him show up. Let Him make the sun stand still!

Another verse I relied heavily on was Matthew 11:28: *Come to me, all you who are weary and burdened, and I will give you rest.* And mommas, may He be exactly who you go to when you are weary and burdened. Let Him be your hiding place. Your resting place.

The emotional breaking point of our adoption, for me, was the night of our referral. At the end of the book, you'll find our story in full. But, here's a quick snapshot. We received our referral on a Thursday night when I was in small group, and my husband was at band practice (for the worship team). My small group took a field trip to church, so my husband and I could open the referral together. We wanted to lay eyes on our children at exactly the same time. Did you catch that word- *children?*

When we opened the referral, we saw the most precious pictures of two little boys. Everyone rejoiced that we were one step closer to bringing our children home. During the opening of our referral and the commute back home, I'd been in correspondence with our adoption agency. As we turned on Main Street, I asked a question and received a response that stole my breath.

- *(Me) Yes, I have the information for our first son, but where's the rest of the information?*

And as I waited for the response, I'm pretty sure my heart stopped.

- *(Agency) You have all of the information there is. What more do you want?*
- *(Me) Where's the information for our second child?*
- *(Agency) No, you have just the one. That is a referral for another family.*

So, all the referrals going out that week were on the same email. And this week, there were only two referrals going out. Each family was growing by one son. We thought both of the boys were ours. You see, we'd requested two children. On all of our paperwork. And in our payments. 2 children. That was the plan. So, at that moment, With that line. In that email. We lost a child. I know- you're thinking- lost a child? Isn't that a little dramatic?

Nah. Not really. By this point, we'd been praying for our children since December 2012. The night of our referral was December 2014. Two years. Two years of praying daily for our children. Then, we got to see our sons' faces. And within minutes, one of those sons was ripped from us. He was no longer ours.

I wept.

We were told we had two options. We could accept the referral of one child or give that referral back and rejoin the waiting list again to wait for two children.

Now, reading this, you may think, you'd cry over this? Really, you felt like you lost a child? That's a little much Kelley. Or, maybe you think, it's a no-brainer- go with the referral now and adopt again later.

But you see, it wasn't that simple. Our hearts had been set that we were bringing home two children. That was the plan. That was how we were going to be obedient to scripture. We were going to do the absolute most and best we could do for the Lord and for these children. So, to hear we were only given one in our referral, we really began to struggle. *Lord, does this mean we need to give this precious child back to you? Is that the ultimate sacrifice? Say goodbye to him now, to welcome two children home later?* It truly was more difficult than a simple yes or no to move forward. And while we did call and consult with all the wise counsel that had supported us each step of the way, it was ultimately our call. It was going to be our act of faith. Not theirs. So, really, nothing they could have said would have given us peace or direction. The result of our decision and the fate of that precious little boy in our referral was ultimately in our hands.

And it was with that understanding, that his life was in our hands, that we said yes to his referral and moved forward with the adoption. Our agency told us that even though all of our paperwork up to this point said two children, we could continue on with just one. It'd simply mean that our paperwork would be good for the next year to begin another adoption since we'd already been approved for two.

The next few days were pretty rough. While I was truly over the moon that we'd made it this far- that we knew who our son was- I was deeply troubled over the loss of our second child.

Mommas, have you been there? When everything you were doing was to be obedient to scripture. To glorify God. And yet, things didn't work out. And there was no good reason. Did you not just feel hurt? Confused? Maybe even a little lost as to what in the world was going on? That's exactly what was going on with me.

As I mentioned earlier, the ride home from receiving the big news was in a car with my some of my closest friends- my small group ladies. Toward the end of the ride home, they'd noticed my joy had begun to wane, and a storm of confusion and discouragement had begun to brew. Later that week, after moving forward with our referral, I'd reached out to a dear friend from group. Basically, I texted that I was miserable and felt like the wind of our adoption sails had been sucked dry.

And she proceeded to put me in my place. She told me to go grab my joy, put it back in my heart because I had work to do. My son was coming home. There were women all around the world that may never get to experience the joy of having even one child. Their Plan A didn't include children. I needed to get my stuff together and be thankful.

Was her pep talk an immediate fix? Not really. But, it did help put my misery into perspective. And mommas, sometimes, that's just what we need. So, what did this momma do? I went to Him. And, you should too. Matthew 11:28: *"Come to me, all you who are weary and burdened, and I will give you rest."*

And dear sweet mommas, before I close this chapter, I must address one more disheartening avenue through which discouragement may come.

It's called: When you mess up.

We already talked about how difficult it can be to accept that other people will be stakeholders in your adoption that you'll never meet, who will determine whether or not your child comes home. And ultimately, that's a fate we just have to accept. There's no way around that fire except straight through it.

But what do we do, how do we respond, when it's our fault things are going wrong?

As I've mentioned, we received our referral through email first in December 2014. We had to go ahead and accept it by email response that we wanted to move forward with our adoption. We were then told we would have the actual referral sent to our house that we would need to forward on to be notarized and eventually sent to Washington, DC.

Well, by now, have you caught on that this was our first adoption? It was kind of a fly by the seat of your pants and figure it out as you go journey. We had no idea what that referral packet would look like. We received no further information from our agency. And, we didn't reach out to other families to ask questions about what the referral would look like, because, as silly as this sounds, we kind of thought we would know it when we saw it. Surely it was going to say "referral" somewhere on the package, right?

It turns out, that's not a thing. Of course, it can't be that easy. Upstairs one morning over winter break, the doorbell rang. Excited, I went downstairs thinking it was going to be our referral. I said a very rushed hello to our FedEx carrier and quickly accepted the package. Upon opening the package, I was discouraged to find that I already had that information. It was all just hard copies of forms we'd already received through email. Thinking nothing more of it, I put the package on our desk and went back upstairs.

About two weeks passed by and I began to question why it was taking so long to receive our referral package. I logged-on to an adoption support group I was a part of and started asking questions. I explained to the group that I'd received a package but didn't see anything about our referral in it or anything that had a place for us to sign that we were accepting the referral specifically. They asked me to list a few of the documents in our package. Once I did, they said they were pretty sure what I had was indeed my referral and that no- there is not a paper that says "Referral."

I lost it. Do you get what this meant? This meant that I'd had my son's referral. For TWO WEEKS. Just sitting on my desk. I'd walked by it for days not realizing it was the key to my son coming home. It just sat there. I'd-unknowingly- acted as if that package was just another stack of papers we'd file away for safekeeping. Life changing documents that I walked by on a daily basis and never gave a second glance.

Let's take it a step further. Because I'd not realized what those documents were, my son had stayed in foster home for TWO EXTRA WEEKS. At that moment, it was my fault. My fault he was there. My fault things weren't moving forward. My fault he wasn't coming home. I'd been going about my week, holding the key to my son's homecoming, while he remained in a foster home. Halfway around the world. Without me. He was without me because I'd failed.

Y'all. I lost it. Fell to my knees. Screamed. Wept. Heaved. I was inconsolable. How do you come back from that? The very thing I was trying to be the solution for, I'd become the problem. I was the cause. Oh, y'all. There's no forgetting that night. It is etched into my mind.

So, what do you do? How do you respond when you've made the mistake? When you've messed up? When you're the cause of your own discouragement and disappointment?

It's pretty simple. You realize you're not in control. You humble yourself and you fall at His feet. And you stay there until you can move. Until you've given it all to Him. You stay there. And when you've surrendered. When He's taken His hand and extended it to yours. When He's whispered *I know. I'm here.* When you hear His voice, you use His strength, and you stand. You get up off your knees, and you stand. And, you say *thank you.* Because His grace is sufficient. His grace is enough.

In 2 Corinthians 12, Paul writes: *9 But he said to me, "My grace is sufficient for you, for my power is made perfect in weakness." Therefore, I will boast all the more gladly about my weaknesses, so that Christ's power may rest on me. 10 That is why, for Christ's sake, I delight in weaknesses, in insults, in hardships, in persecutions, in difficulties. For when I am weak, then I am strong.*

And momma's, that's how we move forward. That's how we adopt. We cannot and will not be able to do this alone. And at times, because by His grace things will be going so well, we'll think we're doing it all. That it's our hard work and diligent effort that's moving things along. But that's not it at all. It's all by His grace that we adopt. It's by His grace we move forward. It's by His grace we live.

Live in His grace.

WELCOME HOME

And we'll see you at work on Monday?

When your welcome home is not all that welcoming.

Our journey through adoption had been incredible. Absolutely incredible. God had shown himself more clearly to us than we had ever seen Him before. People jumped on board with our adoption. People gave. People shared our story. It truly felt like a community adoption, not just a Lambert adoption.

So naturally, I expected the same sentiments any new mom would receive after we got off the plane. Except, that's not what I got.

We landed on my son's birthday. So, of course, the first thing we did was immediately usher our crew over to Chick-Fil-A to celebrate his birthday with fried chicken like all great events should be celebrated. After the cake and presents, it was time to wrap things up. Clearly, we had just been on a two-day journey to come home.

As friends and family headed out the doors, a dear friend - whom I served with weekly at church- made the first of many comments I'd come to receive over the next few weeks, that truly rattled me. "I know you're ready to get back into things, but I'll cover you this week." With that, my friend left, without a second glance. And probably, feeling as if a great favor had just been given.

I, on the other hand, had an immediate response in my head that never made it out of my mouth. I simply responded with, "Okay, thanks." What I wanted to say, and should have said in a polite version was, "Are you crazy?!? I just got home. What happened to my six weeks? The school system I work for at least agreed to give me that. Yes, I've missed you incredible people terribly, and I've definitely missed serving with you each week at church, but really? You're going to cover me for just one Sunday? Today's Saturday. You're saying all I get is one week?"

I struggled to process the reality that just hit me. This dear friend serves faithfully at church every week. And in my absence for the 3 weeks, we were in Africa, this friend filled-in for me. It wasn't a lack of care or sincerity in which the words were offered. Those words were truly offered in the sense of, "I love you. Y'all just got home. Take it easy and rest. I've got you covered this week." Not one ounce of it was, "Man, I'm tired of doing your stuff, you get one more week off, then it's over."

But, in a highly-emotional and even more highly exhausted state, that's how I heard it. And, it hurt. So, here's the part where Chapter 3 comes in big time. Your friends and family simply -most likely- don't have an understanding of adoption. And they won't unless you open your mouth and speak. Was the time to open my mouth those few seconds as my friends slipped out of Chick-Fil-A's doors? No. Definitely not. I wasn't prepared. I was emotional. That wasn't the time. But, that next Sunday at church, was.

I sent a message later that week and explained to essential personnel: "Hey guys. I'm going to be out of serving the next few weeks. Our family will be attending church, but I'm not actually going to check him in just yet (into our Church's children's ministry). I don't want to put him in a setting where he's being left, or in a room full of other children. I don't want him to think he's back at the foster home." Some people responded with a "got it." Others didn't respond.

What did happen, that might just knock your socks off, was the same friend that told me only the next Sunday would be covered, came to me the next Sunday I was back at church and said, "You know, I never really thought of it that way. But now that I have, it really makes sense (why I wasn't serving)." From that day forward, we were able to talk about orphans, adoption, and attachment. Without reservation.

You see, your friends and family haven't experienced adoption. (Most likely.) They haven't thought through the very things that are integral to your child's adaptation and overall well-being. Things like how scary being dropped-off and left with people in a room full of children your child doesn't know could be for your child. Like how some families have to get rid of pets because, at some orphanages, children are told that dogs are vicious animals and will eat them, as a way to manage to keep children in the compound. Or, how some families sleep with the lights on and in the same room for several months once they get home because their child's orphanage kept the lights on at night. So, to be taken from the only home they've ever known and be expected to sleep alone and, in the dark, would be terrifying. Or, how you have to be intentional about who gets to hold your child and when they get to hold him/her because being passed around from person-to-person would seem incredible terrifying. Your child hasn't even figured out y'all are their parents yet. Or, how it would be scary to immediately be enrolled in a school setting because your child would be on the only one of a different ethnicity- or the only one that doesn't speak English.

You have to do everything you can to protect your child. And unfortunately, because you didn't birth this child from your body, you don't look like a family that needs the adjustment period that most new mothers are given without a second thought. After all, you didn't require a hospital stay. So, everybody is healthy, and you're good? Right?

No, not so much, Mom. Not so much, Dad. You must be your child's biggest advocate and biggest protector. Research. Read books. Think things through. What is the adjustment period going to look like for your child? The needs of your child will be different based on every single circumstance surrounding your child's adoption. I highly recommend reading <u>Thriving as an Adoptive Family</u> by David and Renee Sanford. This book will go through what it may look like bringing your child home at all different ages and stages of life. It was a great conversation starter for my husband and I in the three years we waited to bring our son home. It made us think through even the tiniest of details: Should we go ahead and start sleeping with the lights on, so we can get used to it- since it's common for orphanages to keep the lights on at night?

Little prompts like those really started to get our minds wrapped around how different bringing home our child through adoption might actually be, rather than a child I would birth. Those things make a huge difference.

Here's a few things I could have done a lot better with, and I hope you'll take heed to.

- Prepare those in your circles in advance with what it will/may look like when you come home. Had my fellow volunteers known in advance that I would not be serving for a few weeks once our son was home, it would have never become an emotional sore spot for me because we would have already talked about it. It would have also prevented any confusion for our friends. The time we spent having to go over the realities of adoption after the fact, could have been spent sharing all of the amazing things God had done instead.

- Prepare phrases for difficult questions in advance. The hardest thing I experienced after bringing our son home was telling people they couldn't hold him. We stayed home a good bit those first few weeks. But eventually, it was time to journey outside our walls, into the walls of church and our workspaces. Since everyone was so involved in our adoption, everyone couldn't wait to squeeze and hold and love and snuggle the little man who was an orphan no more. He is a big deal to them and they are a part of his story. They had waited so long for the moment to hold him. But in those first few weeks, that moment had to wait. And I had to be the one to tell them that hard truth. Our son was still learning who mom and dad were. He was, for the first time in his life, surrounded by pools of white people. That's new and scary in itself. He was overstimulated, and jet-lagged. Those moments weren't the time to play pass the baby. Be prepared to tell your loved ones *no.*

One moment I deeply regret happened at a cookout at a friend's house. We'd had our son home for a little less than a month. We were sitting on the back deck when one of our friends asked if they could hold him. I freaked out. I loved this person so stinking much, but I already loved my son more, and I knew my son needed the security of my arms. I'd done hours upon hours of adoption research. I had expansive knowledge of why it's important to have the adoptive parents be the sole caregivers for a while after homecoming. But I had no idea how to communicate everything I learned and knew to be true, to the person who also loved our son so stinking much and just wanted to share a hug with the little guy he'd spent so much time praying for. Regretfully, I looked him in the eye and just shook my head no. And it was awkward. And uncomfortable. And if it wasn't for the grace my friend showed me at that moment, my actions could have deeply hurt a friendship that meant so much to me, and to this day, still does.

Y'all, your community loves you so much. Not only that, they love your children so much. They are beyond ready to love them. Show them the grace that my friend lathered upon me. Prepare your community in advance for what it's going to look like when you come home. The last thing you'll need on your shoulders as you're learning to become a new family is fear that you've damaged relationships that God has so richly blessed you with. So, to my dear friend on the deck that night, thank you for the grace you showed me as I was figuring out how to be a good mom and friend all at the same time.

Here are a few ideas to help:

- A few obvious things you can do if your child is younger would be to have your child in an infant carrier or in a stroller. While there are a few, most people aren't bold enough to try and take your child out of a carrier.
- Some people send out invitations to a welcome home party, with specific instructions. *We are so excited to welcome you into our home. We have waited so long for this moment. As we prepare to celebrate this wonderful occasion with you, we hope you'll understand that as much as we can't wait to talk, laugh, and share stories as we pass the potatoes and mac-and-cheese, we won't be passing our son. Right now, we're teaching him who loves him, who is going to provide for him, and who is going to meet his needs. Please help us do this by allowing us to hold him, feed him, and change his diapers. Sooner than we'll be prepared for, he'll walk right up to you and share all of his love with you, that you have so lavishly shared*

> *with our family. Thank you for your understanding.*
- Or, try something to this effect when someone asks if they can hold your child. *Thank you for asking, but we aren't quite ready to let go just yet.*

Remember moms and dads; this is your child. Your responsibility. Your person. You have the right to say no. Exercise that right. Say *no* to nights out. Say *no* to *pass the baby.* Say *no* to anything your family isn't ready for. Just when you do, always explain why. And explain in advance. These people love you. When they understand they are helping you by not holding your child, they'll want to help.

To our community: a thousand thank-yous for all of the grace and love you generously bestowed upon our family throughout our adoption.

AFTER THE PLANE

Busy Beaver.

That's really what you're going to become once you're home. Now, I know you're thinking-*hang on Kelley, I've been busy this whole dagum time. What do you mean I'll be busy after the plane?* Well, I simply mean that the work isn't over yet.

Think about it. There are a lot of decisions and things you've still gotta do. And, in case you aren't thinking about them just yet, now's a good time to get them on your radar.

➤ Doctors' appointments: If you haven't already, go ahead and begin researching doctors. Ask your friends who they recommend. And, even better, if you have an adoptive family in your community, ask them for a recommendation. Doctors have a huge impact on your child's health and your emotional wellbeing.

　　　o　Here's an example: We'd done our research and decided on a pediatrician. We visited her for the first year of our son's homecoming. Well, she moved. So, we had to try out a new doctor. It became SO glaringly obvious with the questions the new doctor was asking us that she had never even looked at our file. She had no idea our son was adopted before we walked in the room and didn't clue into that fact until I told her. Even though my husband is White, I'm White, and our daughter is White, she had not a clue that our African son was not biologically born into our family. Why would it matter? Because- our biological child needs to be meeting health and growth standards for a typical American/White child. Our adopted child needs to be meeting health/growth standards of his birth country. Otherwise, we're diagnosing problems that aren't actually there. Another thing that was super frustrating was an over concern with language development. Of course, my son, who has not been in America where we speak English, is not going to be speaking English words and connecting them in 2-3-word sentences at the same developmental stage of a child who was born in a culture that does speak English. These things became super frustrating. Even just that one appointment. So, know your doctor. If you have to switch doctors, call ahead and make sure the staff puts a note in your child's file for the doctor to review the specifics of your child's case before the appointment.

○ Historical information: Guard your heart mommas when you have to fill out your child's background info. There's a pretty good chance you won't know your child's family history. You probably won't know if there's a history of heart disease or cancer. What you can try and find out, however, is any medical consistencies of the region your child comes from. For example, we were warned specifically about the effects of codeine on children that can be detrimental.

- ○ Surgeries: If you're adopted child is a boy, you may need to consider the positives and negatives of circumcision. Most likely, if you're adopting from an orphanage, your child will not be circumcised. Is this something your family will do? Will your child be past the point of age when it is a recommended procedure? If you are considering it, will your insurance cover it? Go ahead and have those conversations now, so it's not a hot-topic you have to discuss after the fact. Also, if your insurance won't cover it, know that this is a cost you need to plan for.

- ○ Adding your child to your insurance policy: Go ahead and look up what's required: birth certificate, etc. Make sure you know what's needed to enroll your child. This is one more thing you can look into now, to save stress later.

➢ Daycare: As you can imagine, this is a biggie. Really pray about whether you'll stay home, opt for an in-home daycare or a center. While it's not that any one of these may be wrong for your child, there probably will be a best fit. As you read earlier, we didn't want our son going into a setting that could remind him of being in the orphanage. AKA- another room full of children. If you're adopting a toddler, another factor to consider is potty training. Look over their policies on potty training. Adopted children/children in transition can have a higher tendency to regress or be slower to adapt to potty training. They've already had so much change in their lives that adding another change may be too much too soon. Or, the orphanage may not have even started potty training, so you may be starting from scratch. So, just look over their policies to know where you stand.

➤ School: If your child is a little bit older, you may actually be looking at schools. It's always good to consider diversity when you're looking at schools. It's also a good idea to look at their Exceptional Needs programs. What accommodations are they prepared to make? Could they place your child in a grade that better suits their learning needs, instead of just focusing on your child's age for placement?

➤ Paperwork: Now that your child is home, or you have your child with you, the paperwork is going to get so much easier. Seriously momma. Find your comfiest chair. Sit down. Say *woooooh.* Cause the hard part is over. While you take a load off, here are a few things I do want to put on your radar for the next few months:

  o Contact your home study agent to complete your post adoption report. This usually needs to be filed within the first month. For some agencies, you may have up to three months before it needs to be filed. Typically, you have to file formal reports at 1-3, 6, and 12 months home. For our adoption, we also have to send in reports once a year until he's 18. Fortunately, we can type these up ourselves.

○ Apply for your child's social security card. It's not hard. Each state has different requirements, but it's usually stuff you already have. Things like: passport, birth certificate, contract of adoption, certificate of citizenship. Will you definitely need those exact papers? No, but just know, don't stress about this step. It's literally a matter of gathering the stuff you already have and going to the social security office. You do all of it at their little window. You don't even need to go into one of their conference rooms. Some states even allow you to make appointments, so there won't be a wait at all!

○ Readoption: Now hear me loud and clear mommas, all states do not require this step. It's often optional. However, depending on the type of visa your child came into the country with (international adoptions), you may be required to readopt. The beauty of readoption is it gives your child a state birth certificate and if a name change is necessary, the redoption paperwork handles this. It also changes your status of being a legal guardian, to being their parent. That can be significant when it comes time for college scholarships.

  ■ You may be able to handle the readoption yourself. You may not. We did. Our post-placement agency was incredible. They sent us a link to all of the forms required. We printed them off and filled them out. They had to send in 2 of the post-adoption reports they'd already completed and fill-out a form or two. They sent that stuff directly to the courthouse for us and we brought the other forms. We were able to complete the readoption for about $150. A lawyer typically starts charging around $1,500. If it makes you more comfortable having them handle everything for you, absolutely hire a lawyer. However, it is possible to do it yourself.

One thing I absolutely loved about our son's readoption was that the whole family got to be there. This was super important and super special since they couldn't attend in Africa. Think about it- usually, when a mom gives birth to a child, the whole family comes to the hospital to *ooh* and *awww.* Everyone is there to celebrate your little one's arrival and give thanks to God for all He has done. They don't get this opportunity when you're in a different state or a different country. Your child's arrival is a big deal. If you can have a readoption celebration, do it. If you're allowed to have a packed courthouse, do it! God has done a mighty thing in your lives and your child is crazy special and important, so take the opportunity. Take the moment. Invite everyone. Praise God for His goodness.

NEGATIVE NANCY

Avoid her like the plague.

Oh, Mommas. Sometimes, Negative Nancy is just dying to come out. I mean, ready. Give her a microphone and she'll go to town. But you know what, she's not your friend. She, in fact, is an enemy and can ruin your adoption if you let her. If you make friends with her. Or, if you choose to be her.

Have you ever been around *that* person? You know, the one who is always going to find a way to spin something negatively. Or, is just plain and simple always negative? Don't you normally try to avoid her like the plague? In fact, if you see her walking down the hall, you might even slip into the restroom just to avoid whatever drama she's ready to unload. And what's crazy is that you actually like Nancy. She knows her stuff. What she says is usually true. And you know that if anyone is going to tell you like it is, it's going to be Nancy. She's not a bad person. Not at all. It's just that she brings you down.

Dear friend, you are going to have opportunity after opportunity to not only do a meet and greet with Negative Nancy, you'll have many opportunities to become Negative Nancy. Adoption is hard. Many parts are unreasonable and outrageous. So much of adoption is eight-thousand times harder than it really ever needs to be. And heaven knows it takes 20 years longer than it should. But you know what, don't we all know those things already? In fact, don't most people already know those things about adoption? I'd even go as far to say that those very things are the reasons why more people aren't adopting.

You know what? Even if you do a marvelous job at not personally becoming Nancy or even her slightly-less offensive cousin, you're definitely going to meet her, often. Here's how this will go down:

You are out to dinner with friends. After the usual catch-up and weather hullabaloo, someone will ask how the adoption's going. Speaking honestly, you'll reply that either things are delayed due to a paperwork issue, or you're in the middle of waiting for an update (which you've been doing for months now). Let's take a minute here just to clarify- all you've done is said exactly what's happening. You haven't cried. You haven't shouted. You haven't exaggerated. You haven't even batted an eye. You've simply shared what's going on with your story because they asked.

Before you can share anymore about your adoption, your table companions speak up. *"This is just ridiculous. I can't believe they are doing that to these children, keeping them in orphanages. Don't they know these children need homes? I mean really. You've been in this process for how long now? This is just ridiculous. I'd be so upset if I were you. I don't know how you do it. How much have you paid? It's several thousand, right? And they still can't move your paperwork along? Who is your senator? We need to email him right now!"* And all you did was state the facts.

People, especially those that love and care for you, are ready to lay on the righteous anger and lay it on thick! Here's what I'm telling you: You don't need to share the drama and saga about all the difficult parts of adoption. Everyone already knows it. In fact, they are waiting to hear it from you. **And when you don't pitch in and get all fussy, it shakes them.** It rattles them. When you start explaining that- *if this were your child, you'd want this process. You'd hope and pray that if you had to make the toughest decision of your life and orphan your child, that you'd hope your child's adoptive parents would have* *to go through rigorous screening and pay substantial amounts of money because your child's life is so incredibly important. That though their name may now hold orphan next to it, they were first and foremost your child and that gives them value. You get the wait. You get it's tough. Could the process be better and perhaps streamlined? Oh, yeah! But is it worth it? Absolutely. Would you do every bit of it all over again? No doubt in your mind! You'd never think twice.* - they won't have a negative word left.

THAT RESPONSE? That is radical. That's counter-cultural. That's thought evoking. That's a game changer. Dear momma, on your toughest days, please oh please oh please, bookmark this page. Come back and read it. Remember that your child's birth mom made the most difficult decision of her life and because of it, your life will be abundantly blessed. Her most significant loss became your best gain. Don't lose perspective. Earn the right to be your child's mom. If you don't believe that your child is worth this process, then why on earth are you adopting?

So, ignore Nancy. And if you get the chance, don't become her.

Become her. Say what?!? You mean me? Yes. I mean you. It's totally possible. It happens often and sometimes unintentionally. One of the things I'll mention later on and have already alluded to how important community is throughout your adoption. Community, for a lot of people, is found online through groups and social media platforms. Through such a context, I learned a lot about the importance of our tongue as it is referred to in the book of James. Over the course of a few years, I followed a couple in their process of adoption. They were super well-loved and well respected in their community. Great people. Truly great people. Plugged into church. Huge heart for orphans and widows. Mission trips. Like. Really good people. Right? Keep in mind, all aspects of my positive opinion of them was formed almost solely through social media.

Well, after the excitement of their "we're adopting" post, I began noticing some really negative things getting posted online. Any time anything went wrong with their adoption, it was immediately posted. Like- within minutes. If someone didn't buy tickets to support their fundraiser, there'd be comments online like, "I just don't understand how people could not buy a ticket to support our adoption. Do they not love orphans? Jesus? I just don't understand how they can be so cold hearted?"

Now, hold the phone. Cold hearted? For real? Momma, haven't you ever walked into Walmart, seen the table of girl scouts and their noteworthy cookies, and kept walking? Not because you think their cookies are horrible- because we all know they taste good. We all know girl scouts are a good cause. You simply kept on walking because honest-to-goodness, you didn't have $5. You were maxed out. You were buying generic version of everything. You bought the cheapest toilet paper. You bought the discount toothpaste. You didn't have $5. It **wasn't because you hated girl scouts or didn't want them to succeed.**

-So, remember this- when people don't give- when they don't buy a ticket for your fundraiser- when they don't buy a shirt- it's not because they don't want to help you. It's not because they hate orphans or don't love Jesus. It's really likely that they simply don't have any extra money. And in the chance that you encounter someone who wants to give but tells you things are tight- ask them to share your story- literally. They could repost on social media. Or, they could ask their pastor if you could share your story at the end of a sermon. Or, they could arrange a women's brunch at their house- where you bring the food and the story. Or, they could invite you to share your story at their small-group. There are a thousand ways people can plug-in. Just remember. **Just because they don't give financially, doesn't mean they can't get involved. And it definitely does not mean they don't love Jesus.**

This adoptive momma continued to post really discouraging things about their adoption experience. Things that, honestly, weren't unique to them. Things like paperwork errors and the cost of adoption. She even started posting about conversations she had with people that had turned south. Conversations like, "Why would you adopt a black kid?" *Now, I could take this moment to address how ridiculous this statement is, but that's not the point of this chapter. Just remember- these are His children. That's all that matters.* She would be quick to jump online and use social media as her bullhorn for all of the stupid and judgmental things ignorant people said to her. Unfortunately, instead of using those moments as opportunities to change perspectives, she often used those moments as gripe sessions. It began to seem like it was the whole world vs. her adoption. It got ugly.

And you know what came from that? A really discouraged momma. Actually, not just one. Not just her. I became discouraged, too. I started thinking; *surely, it's not going to be that bad for us? That's not possible, right?* It was really tough reading all they were going through. Was I naive enough to think those bad things weren't going to happen to us? No, of course not. But, it did begin to place unnecessary seeds of doubt. Things like- *Why is God letting them go through all of this? He could make it easier, couldn't he? Why is He letting this happen?* It made me begin to question all of the things I already knew about God. And that, dear momma, is not the influence you want to have on someone else.

So, aside from 2 really discouraged mommas, what else came from her penchant to be a Negative Nancy? Not much besides an ever-evolving image of this dear adoptive momma. What do I mean? Well, most likely, people read her posts and instead of being moved to adopt or get involved with her adoption, they began to form an opinion of her. It probably went something like this:

1. Person logs-on to Facebook.

2. Person sees her post.

3. Person is appalled at the things others are saying to her.

4. Person's eyes get real big as they read her response to what others are saying.

5. Person thinks to himself: *Wow, she's really upset. I wouldn't mess with her. She seems really angry. Adoption must be super hard. She's a strong person for sticking with it. Especially since people can be so mean. Good for her.*

Most likely, no one read her rants and thought: *Gee, adoption sounds like such a good idea. God really provides. He's really taking care of her.*

Now, did she ever post about the power of God and all the good things He did in their adoption? Oh yeah. Absolutely. But, is that what's memorable? No. I heard it said once, *if we would elevate our blessings as much as we elevate our problems, the world would be a much happier place.* Ain't that truth? What a good word!

You won't possibly complete an adoption without the power of God. So, tell that story. Get people to pray for you. Sure, share your hardships and struggles. But, do so without complaining. Ask for prayer. Give updates. And when God does something BIG, and He WILL, that's when you use social media as your bullhorn and go to town! Remember, adoption is His story. His idea. He created it.

Don't be the reason more people aren't adopting. We know it's hard. They know it's hard. But we know it's worth it. There's no need to dwell on the tough parts of adoption. Doing that... well it won't change anything. Actually, that's not true. It will make everything and everyone more miserable.

So, when you get the chance to be Nancy, don't. Instead, do this:

1 Thessalonians 5:16-18: *Rejoice always, pray without ceasing, give thanks in all circumstances; for this is the will of God in Christ Jesus for you.*

And if times are really hard, which we all know they're bound to be at some point, keep the Lord's Word in front of you. Think about the book of James. If that much of a book of the Bible is dedicated to how we speak and having control over our tongues, the implication there must be that what we say really does matter.

James 1:19-20: *My dear brothers and sisters, take note of this: Everyone should be quick to listen, slow to speak and slow to become angry, because human anger does not produce the righteousness that God desire.* In other words, as soon as something doesn't go your way, don't hop on social media and blab about it. Listen to what's going on. Take time to figure out the solution or the steps to a possible solution.

Take the time to read this excerpt from James 3:3-12:

3 When we put bits into the mouths of horses to make them obey us, we can turn the whole animal. 4 Or take ships as an example. Although they are so large and are driven by strong winds, they are steered by a very small rudder wherever the pilot wants to go. 5 Likewise, the tongue is a small part of the body, but it makes great boasts. Consider what a great forest is set on fire by a small spark. 6 The tongue also is a fire, a world of evil among the parts of the body. It corrupts the whole body, sets the whole course of one's life on fire, and is itself set on fire by hell.

7 All kinds of animals, birds, reptiles and sea creatures are being tamed and have been tamed by mankind, 8 but no human being can tame the tongue. It is a restless evil, full of deadly poison.

9 With the tongue we praise our Lord and Father, and with it we curse human beings, who have been made in God's likeness. 10 Out of the same mouth come praise and cursing. My brothers and sisters, this should not be. 11 Can both fresh water and salt water flow from the same spring? 12 My brothers and sisters, can a fig tree bear olives, or a grapevine bear figs? Neither can a salt spring produce fresh water.

Can we put a different spin on how we use social media and interact with our communities? What if we used what God's doing in our adoptions as an opportunity to be a reprieve for our followers from the typical negative mommy posts? What if we radically changed the culture of mommy posting? Instead of moms posting online about how tired they are because their husbands don't help out around the house and their kids won't listen, and everybody is judging the way they parent, they began posting about God's grace in parenting and marriage? Holy cow. Isn't that a newsfeed you'd want to read? You wouldn't have to go to bed every night thinking- *gee I'm so lucky my husband isn't cheating on me like so-and-so's husband.* You'd go to bed thinking, *hey- I saw Jim and Suzie posted about how great it was to set-up a mommy-daddy date night once a week. I bet that's something we could probably do. Maybe we could go in together for a babysitter?* That's just flying off the cuff. But, what if, just what if, our posts inspired other moms to seek righteousness in the everyday mundane and hullabaloo?

Can I take it one step further? What if our posts and the ways we interacted with our community inspired someone else to adopt or foster? What if God uses our responses and our story to reveal to someone else that taking care of vulnerable children is their Plan A? In our story, glory to God alone, that very thing happened.

Our adoption story, which is ever evolving, began with our hearts readied for adoption in December of 2012 and our son coming home in August 2015. We didn't see our son's face or know of his existence until December 4, 2014. That means, we did community with people for two years before we were introduced to our son. That's a lot. A lot of:

- fundraising with community
- praying with community
- going to church with community
- keeping our community up-to-date on the steps in our adoption
- praising God for what He was doing in our adoption, with our community

One Sunday, before we received our referral, a friend at church said she would like to watch our children for free when they came home. She knew that we were concerned about putting them in full-time daycare and felt like God was moving in her heart to watch our kids. Can you say AMEN and HALLELUJAH?!?

Side note- this is the very same person my husband and I had been hoping God would make a way for her to watch our kids. Y'all, God knows what's going on. He's in the details.

Fast forward a year to when our son comes home, and we have to go to work. She takes care of our son from October of 2015 through June of 2016. In the spring of 2016, she walked us out to my car and said, *I think we're going to foster. We've seen your son and the love you have for him. Y'all are a family. We can do it, too.*

And. They. Did.

They become foster parents because of the great work that God did in our lives. That's why we share our story. When God works, He works radically. He does things bigger and ten times better than you could have ever imagined them. When you share your family's adoption story, don't share the negative woes of adoption. Share HIS story. Share what HE is doing. Share how you have peace in the overwhelming. How you have found hope in the dead of night. How He is the joy. That He is WHY WE ADOPT.

There's a song by Andy and Rachel Graham from their album *Vision in the Wild*. Within the song are these beautiful lyrics.

> *I've found peace in the overwhelming*
> *You speak life in the dead of night*
> *You're the hope that holds the future*
> *Faithful God, faithful Father*

Dear adoptive mommas, I pray that verse over you. That you'd find peace in the overwhelming and that you'd know the One who speaks in the dead of night and rest in His Hope that holds the future.

Before we close this chapter, let's address one more thing: international vs. domestic adoption. Because, no matter what side of the fence you're on, you're going to receive criticism for it. If you're adopting internationally, Negative Nancy is going to ask you, "But, what about all the kids here? Don't they matter? Shouldn't we take care of them before worrying about others?"

Negative Nancy popped up for us on Facebook over the international vs. domestic debate. It went something like this: "Kelley, why don't you adopt from our country? Don't these kids matter?" Now, let me set the stage for you: At this point, we'd already posted SEVERAL adoption videos. We'd thrown multiple yard sales. We'd sent off applications. Done our home study. We were pretty far in the trenches of paperwork for international adoption. And now she's gonna ask that. Are we for real? And on FACEBOOK. Come on.

But you see, that's what they do. Nancies are everywhere. And remember what I said earlier- they mean well. They don't intend harm. They just see things one way and have a hard time imagining a different perspective. But here's the beauty of when a Nancy approaches you with a phrase like, "I just don't understand..." or "Why would....". That's your God-given opportunity to share the WHY of adoption. So, that's exactly what I did.

My response went something like this: *Thanks so much for asking. For Chase and me, we want to be very obedient to scripture and we know His word calls us to take care of orphans. (James 1:27.) Well, it also says to take His gospel to the ends of the earth. (Acts 1:8) and to let the children come to Him (Luke 18:16). So, when we paired these scriptures together, we really began to understand that adoption has no address- that all of the orphans- everywhere- are important to Him.*

And, that was pretty much it. She responded with a-*yeah, okay.* But I tell you what, I had several people that came up to me and said they'd seen her post on my wall and were wondering what I was going to say to that. You see momma's- we all know Negative Nancies. And, we all buck up when a Nancy directs her negativity toward another momma. Well, all my momma friends were watching and waiting to see how I was going to respond. And with that response, they were really proud. They were wondering if I was going to come out with my claws out and rip her apart because after all- *how dare she judge me for adopting internationally when she ain't even adopting locally? Come on now!* But isn't that how we think? Isn't that our gut-go-to? And I could have posted something of that sort- like a- *When you adopt and become an expert on adoption, then come see me*- but how would that have helped? Would that have broadened her perspective? Would that have encouraged anyone else already considering adoption? Would it have encouraged me? No… Responding like that would have just made me a Negative Nancy and that's how I would have spent the rest of the day- really negative.

So, let me say this, just one more time- when you have the chance- or should I say *the choice* to become a Negative Nancy, don't. Be an encourager. Be an inspirer. Share His light. Share His gospel. And who knows, someone else might just adopt because they see what great things He's done in your life.

FUNDRAISING

Because you'll read this chapter first.

I totally nailed that, right? You're most likely in the bookstore debating which book to get. You're holding this book, and you like everything you see, but now that you realize this book comes with a fundraising chapter, you realize you just hit a goldmine! I know! (Said with the enthusiasm of Monica from "Friends.")

Before I get down to the nitty-gritty of how to raise $30,000 or more, there's a lot more that you need to know first. Especially if you don't want to end up getting a second mortgage on your house or taking out more loans.

Fundraising. Your fundraising will only be successful if you heed the wisdom laid out in the previous chapter. No one will ever get on your financial boat if all you do is complain. If you decide to be Negative Nancy, you will undoubtedly sink your ship. How do I know? I've seen it happen. More than once. You can have the most compelling argument for the importance of adoption, but that won't matter. Nearly everyone will agree that the growing number of orphans we have in the world is indeed a crisis of epic proportions. However, if you haven't noticed, very few people are stepping up to be the solution. Why? Because of the negative aura that pro-adoptive people unfortunately put out. If you decide to be Negative Nancy, then don't bother reading this chapter. However, if you heed the advice laid out in the last chapter, then by all means, please keep on reading.

When you're ready to begin fundraising, the first thing you need to do is look at the payment plan your placing agency provided you with. If you don't have one, ask for it now. This will help you decide which fundraisers to do and when. Don't throw this paper away. You'll want to keep it as a reference for your taxes.

**Keep every check. I recommend going ahead now and making a google document that has the following categories: Check number. Check date. Check amount. Purpose. This will come in so handy when it's time for taxes, especially if you're one of the lucky ones that gets audited. Sense my sarcasm? **

Your next step is to determine what expenses are not included in your payment plan and add those costs in to provide yourself with a fundraising goal of total expenses. Here are a few things that may not be included in your agency's payment plan that you may need to account for:

- Background checks for each member in the household: State and Federal (State fingerprinting cards are usually done at your main police department and the federal scans can be done at a live scan center. Often, packaging stores like UPS can provide this service for you. Both of these services can cost between $10 - $50 per person.)

- Medical appointments for home study approval (Usually, your copay). If you have had a physical or seen your physician within the last year, it's possible they will allow you to drop your paperwork off and fill-it-out without requiring an appointment. However, most places now charge a form-fee of $25 to complete paperwork.

- Fingerprinting at a USCIS center (up to $800).

- Document certification: Each document you have will likely need a local notary and state certification.

    - Local Notary: If you have any connections with a local notary, go ahead and ask if you can buy him/her dinner. Ours was a life saver! So many times, we'd realize a tiny mistake and need something resealed before we sent it off. It was an incredible blessing to be able to run over to our notary's house in the wee hours of the night and get that stuff done. Ask around for a connection to a notary, before you pay for one. Side note- most banks will notarize things for you as well and sometimes for free!

- State Certification: Your state's fee will have a huge impact on this. For example, we had to get our marriage and birth certificates certified in SC. Each document was $2 a piece. North Carolina, on the other hand, where we submitted our other thousands of documents, was $10 a piece. Check your state's current certification fee and then multiply that by at least 30. That'll give you a decent estimate to work with.

- Courier fees: Your agency may require you to go ahead and get a FedEx or UPS account. Even if that's not the case, go ahead and budget this in. You're going to be sending thick packets back and forth to your agency and if you're anything like us, you'll want your documents to get there ASAP! Therefore, you're looking at anywhere from $30-80 to send one packet. I would plan to send at least 6 packets.

- Foster care fees/Birth Mom fees: When you receive and accept your referral, your agency may charge you for the care of your child. This may in fact be the happiest money you've ever spent- it's the first time your money directly cares for your child. Woo Hoo! We loved writing these checks. Your agency should be able to recommend a general time frame for how long you need to budget for these fees depending on how long your agency/country moves from referral to home. Even if your agency is super fast and can move this paperwork within three months, you are likely still looking at $1,000 or more just for that short amount of time.   Ours was $400 a month. Remember to multiply this number if you're adopting more than one child. In the case of the birth mom, it's likely you may be paying her hospital and doctor bills depending on what point in her pregnancy/ adoption you are referred to each other.

- Travel: [international and possibly stateside] Ask your agency how many times you are required to travel. Some countries require you to stay between court and embassy, others prefer you to make two separate trips. If that's the case, you're looking at 2 round trip tickets and 4 if you're married. This will add up.

  - Travel Plug: I highly recommend you contact Adoption Airfare. They coordinated all of our travel and left us stress free. Even when canceling and changing flights at the last minute, they handle everything at no-cost to you. We got a call on a Thursday at 1pm and were asked to be in Ethiopia by the next day at 2:30 pm. While I had no idea if that was possible, I immediately got on the phone with Adoption Airfare and they literally checked every airport in the nation to determine if there was anywhere we could depart from and make it. They also handled coordinating our travel on the way home. We obviously couldn't book flights in advance since we didn't know how long court proceedings and document collection would take. While in Africa, I always got an email response within 2 hours, which was incredible considering the time difference! I promise. Contact them now. You'll love them. They're just so nice!

- In-country accommodation expenses: This will vary highly on your type adoption: domestic vs. international and will also vary among countries. Another factor that will impact this expense is how many trips you make and the longevity of each trip. Your agency may have a guest house for you to stay in. If so, go ahead and ask for those fees and if meals are provided within those costs. If not, ask for the hotel information they plan to accommodate you with. Check their nightly accommodations and then add-in money for each meal you'll have to buy. Another thought here is whether or not you'll need laundry services. Some places may charge by article of clothing. If you're there for a while, this could add up too. We just washed our clothes in the tub, but you may not be down for that. If you plan on sight-seeing, buying groceries, buying diapers, going to the market for souvenirs, or eating out, that's all money that needs to be factored in-including money for taxi fare. And remember to note the rate of exchange. That is likely to highly impact the amount of cash you take.

• In-country filing fee expenses: While you probably won't be surprised, I don't want you to be taken off-guard. It's very likely that you will have several last-minute expenses in-country. A fee to file this paper or a fee to file that paper. Or, a form that your agency forgot to tell you about that will be several hundred dollars when you submit it. It happens. Plan ahead. At least plan for your visa fees and your child's visa and passport fees.

Here's something HUGE: Keep an eye on all of your paperwork and their dates. We had to update our paperwork to keep it current. That meant redoing everything- from background clearances to updating the home study and then getting it all notarized and certified again. That was an additional cost we never saw coming. I highly recommend making a master spreadsheet with the titles of your documents and the dates they were created. Most documents expire within 12-18 months. When you start approaching the one-year mark, check with your agency to see if you need to go ahead and start updating everything.

Once you tally all of these additional expenses and any others recommended by your agency, then you're ready to set your fundraising goal. We set ours at $30,000 and by the grace of God alone, we surpassed it! He knew we needed it! How did this happen?

#1 We committed to avoiding Negative Nancy.

#2 We worked real hard and prayed even harder.

#3 Had faith: If it's God's will, it's God's bill!

Fundraising Ideas- Things we did that were successful.

• Yard sales. I know. You knew this one, right? Did you know you can seriously make bank at a yard sale when you partner with a local business or church? If you're involved with a church or a small group, ask them if they'd be willing to have your adoption be their ministry for the month/week by sponsoring your yard sale and having the way their members serve be by donating their items. We had three yard sales and made around $2,500 total. That doesn't suck! Make Facebook posts around time for spring cleaning and Christmas and encourage them to donate to your adoption instead of Goodwill. It can go something like this:

• Ready to make some space in your closet? Donate it to the Smith's yard sale and help us bring our kids home!

or

• Did you know that there are an estimated 157 million orphans worldwide? Would you like to be a part of the solution? It's easy! The Smiths are adopting. Donate your gently used goods to their yard sale to help them bring their children home.

We kept a fundraising thermometer at our yard sale where everyone could see it. We kept track of our profits by adding to the thermometer as the yard sale progressed.

Plus, it helped us encourage people to give us the asking price instead of trying to barter for lower prices.

You'll get a lot of clothing donations most likely. Have a stack of grocery bags and let people fill them for $5. Offer-up, Craigslist, and Facebook are great ways to market your yard sale.

• Puzzle Pieces. Select a puzzle or have one made. A world map puzzle is a solid choice or a puzzle of the country you're adopting from. Choose the amount you want to raise from the fundraiser. For example, if you want to raise $1,000, then "sell" puzzle pieces for $10 each if the puzzle has 100 pieces. This is a really simple fundraiser. It takes virtually no time. And it can all be done on social media. All you have to do is record the name of the person sponsoring a piece of the puzzle on the back of the piece and then put it together. I recommend being strategic about how you build the puzzle as pieces are bought/sponsored. That way, you can add snapshot updates of how the puzzle is coming together and encourage donation drives like this: *Only three more pieces to go and the border will be complete. Will you donate $30 to sponsor these three pieces and help us bring our child home?* Or you could make the puzzle upside down and turn pieces over as they are purchased.

• T-shirts. If you have a slogan for your adoption, now's the time to put that to use. Ours was: love. redemption. adoption. Therefore, that's what our shirts said. Most people wear shirts, so this is one of the best fundraisers you can do since they'll be getting something in return for donating. Most people will bite with this fundraiser. I recommend selling them for at least $20. Don't feel like you have to use an online company either. There's probably a local printing company that would like to partner with your adoption.

- Concert. If there's a music venue, have a concert. Get a local band together, charge admission, that's it. This was one of our favorite fundraisers. It was just fun. Literally, all we had to do was show up. The band does the rehearsing and performing. The only fee we had to pay was for the venue's door guy, so he would get paid. We also set-up a booth and sold t-shirts. There should be a venue in your area that will jump on board once you explain what you're doing. It's great publicity for them to support a local family and it's a tax write-off. Win for everybody!

- Adoption Gala. Now this one was not so easy, but we did raise over $3,000 for this one event. So, totally worth it and it's fun to get all dressed-up! Amazingly generous friends of ours donated the use of their country club, and by donated, I mean paid for the use of their ballroom and had horderves catered. This is one of those events I still look back on and go, "Holy cow. That really happened. A family literally paid for our gala." Don't tell me God isn't good. I'd never believe you.

    - Remember. God has prepared everything in advance for your adoption. Including the community around you. This was His plan A for you. He's got every detail worked out. Down to the people that are going to come alongside you and help you bring your children home.

We had a silent auction, dancing, food, games, and Chase and I spoke. We sold tickets in advance for $25 a piece. People could also pay at the door. I had a few friends that helped me get items for the silent auction-which is surprisingly easy. You just gotta get out there and ask people. Remember, people like giving to a good cause. Give them the opportunity. Ask them. People to ask are local photographers, local restaurants, massage places, and local artists. For games, we did a wine-ring toss. People pay money, get a few rings to toss, and try to get a ring on the neck of a wine bottle. If they ring the bottle, they get to take the wine home. We charged $5 for 3 rings. Note here: this game is not easy. We ended up giving bottles away at the end of the night because we didn't want to take two cases of wine home. Keep in mind, you don't need to have full wine bottles. The bottles can be glued to a mat and if they ring the bottle, they get a prize bag instead of a bottle of wine. We had a cake. It was gorgeous and tasty. If you've got a talented baker friend, they'll likely be thrilled to donate a cake. About 45 minutes into the event, we announced the first winners of the silent auction and then began speaking. This is a crucial time to cast vision about the importance of adoption. Likely, most of your guests brought a date. Chances are, their dates haven't met you and have only heard snippets of your story. You have the opportunity and responsibility to share your story and encourage them to not only get on board by financially sponsoring your adoption by participating in the games and auction, but also by considering adoption for their family. At the end, we danced. It was awesome. Someone even proposed. How can you top that?!?

- SUPER FUN FACT: The couple that got engaged at our gala, is now married, and wait for it…. THEY HAVE ADOPTED THEIR FIRST CHILD!

- Super Bowl Drive. We totally took advantage of everyone being on social media the night of the big game. We did a $30 challenge and included lots of stats about adoption. People gave like crazy. We kept updating the amount that was coming in throughout the night to extend the opportunity for people to get involved. By doing this, our adoption stayed at the top of their newsfeed. And hopefully, on their hearts.

- Videos. We created videos for our "Big Moments." We wanted to actually tell our story, instead of just posting it. Our videos received a lot of positive feedback and helped us drive towards fundraising goals. They were super easy for people to share with their social media connections. As a result, we ended up with a ton of $10 and $25 gifts from acquaintances and friends of friends. Every dime adds up. This is another great opportunity to connect with any media and technology inclined friends you have. They might just be eager to serve your family in this capacity. For us, it was a blessing that this was one small detail that we didn't have to spend hours dwelling over.

Things we didn't do, but you can.

- Baby bottles. Distribute baby bottles to anyone willing to participate. With the bottle, have a short bio and picture. Encourage people to donate to your adoption by filling the bottle with coins. This one is super easy. After all, everyone has to put their loose coins somewhere. Now, you've given them a good cause to donate to.
- Christmas Trees. Know a Christmas, Tree farmer? Ask them if they'd be willing to partner with you to bring your kids home. How can they do this? By allowing a portion of the profits from each tree to be donated to you when the customer mentions your story. Surprisingly, this one might earn you a pretty penny. The same concept can be used with Poinsettias.

- Meal Tickets: Similar to the Christmas Trees, partner with a local food establishment. You're likely to have good traction with a "Mama's Kitchen" or anything family-owned. You'll presale tickets for a set amount ($10 is reasonable). You'll coordinate a date for pick-up with the restaurant and then personally distribute those dinners, or the restaurant may allow the customers to present their tickets at the establishment.

Want to take this one a step farther? Invite business and organizations to partner with your adoption by donating meals to a homeless shelter. By doing this, they can get a great tax write-off and a potential write-up in a local newspaper for how they helped bring your children home and feed the homeless. Win. Win.

SHAMELESS AUDACITY

Pray big prayers.

> Luke 17:6: *He replied, "If you have faith as small as a mustard seed, you can say to this mulberry tree, 'Be uprooted and planted in the sea,' and it will obey you."*

If we're being honest, can we all just admit that sometimes we have no clue what in the world we should pray? Like, for real. Should we ask for specific things or should we sum everything up with a *your will be done.* Do we pray that someone gives a check for exactly the amount we need, or do we just pray that He provides financially? Does asking for something more than once demonstrate a lack of faith? If we ask repetitively, does that mean we didn't trust God to hear us the first time we asked? And then, if we're being, even more, real- how do we explain things to our non-Christian friends whom we're trying to witness to when God doesn't do the big things like we've asked?

Thankfully, God gives us a pretty clear outline in how to pray and how to respond to His answers to our prayers. Check it out:

How we should pray:

> Luke 11:1-13: *One day Jesus was praying in a certain place. When he finished, one of his disciples said to him, "Lord, teach us to pray, just as John taught his disciples."2 He said to them, "When you pray, say:"'Father, hallowed be your name, your kingdom come. 3 Give us each day our daily bread. 4 Forgive us our sins, for we also forgive everyone who sins against us.[c] And lead*

us not into temptation.'" 5 Then Jesus said to them, "Suppose you have a friend, and you go to him at midnight and say, 'Friend, lend me three loaves of bread; 6 a friend of mine on a journey has come to me, and I have no food to offer him.' 7 And suppose the one inside answers, 'Don't bother me. The door is already locked, and my children and I are in bed. I can't get up and give you anything.' 8 I tell you, even though he will not get up and give you the bread because of friendship, yet because of your shameless audacity he will surely get up and give you as much as you need. 9 "So I say to you: Ask and it will be given to you; seek and you will find; knock and the door will be opened to you. 10 For everyone who asks receives; the one who seeks finds; and to the one who knocks, the door will be opened."

I know. I know. This is a text you've heard over and over and over. But, there's something you may have missed here. Yes, this text gives us The Lord's Prayer. But that's not all. It also tells us how to pray in all other areas of life, too. Let's set the stage:

- It's midnight.

- You're dog tired. Kids are in bed. TV is off. You're snoozing.

- Somebody starts banging on your door.

- It's your neighbor. He wants some bread.

- You're so tired you don't even open the door. You just tell him to go away.

- He doesn't leave.

- He bams again.

- You tell him to go away. Again.

- o It's silent for a minute.

- o You go back upstairs.

- o Just as you get under the covers, he starts bamming again.

- o You go downstairs. Open your pantry. Get some bread. Open the door. Shove it in his face. And go back to bed.

That's the scene that's laid out in scripture. I love the way the scriptures describe the neighbor's actions- *shameless audacity.* He would not stop. He kept on bamming. He kept on knocking until he received what he came for. THAT'S how scripture tells us to pray. That annoying, non-stop, repetitive, audacious knocking. Pray like that. Be incessant. And you know what scripture says will happen? It says YOU WILL RECEIVE. That's a promise. From the Word of God. It's a promise from God. So, mommas pray like that. Lean on God's promise to receive.

Proverbs 3:5-6 even tells you to lean on His promises. *Trust in the Lord with all your heart and lean not on your own understanding; 6 in all your ways submit to him, and he will make your paths straight.*[6]

How can you submit to Him? How can you show you trust Him? Do what His Word says. Show your trust and submission by praying like He tells us to pray. Non-stop. With audacious shamelessness.

Now, while we'd all like to leave it at that- *ask and it will be given.* We have to be prudent to read scripture in its entirety and in context. Let's read how that section of the Gospel ends.

➤ Luke 11:11-13: *"Which of you fathers, if your son asks for[f] a fish, will give him a snake instead? 12*

---

[6] Proverbs 3:6 Or *will direct your paths*

Or if he asks for an egg, will give him a scorpion? 13 If you then, though you are evil, know how to give good gifts to your children, how much more will your Father in heaven give the Holy Spirit to those who ask him!"

This text is the ultimate reminder that God is God-thank God- and we are not. It's the reminder that we truly don't know what's best for us. We can't see the big picture. We must put our faith in Him and trust His word when He says, "*how much more will your Father in heaven give the Holy Spirit to those who ask him!*" Meaning, what He's going to do- how He's going to answer our prayers, is way better than we could ever imagine.

➤ Ephesians 3: 20-21: *Now to him who is able to do immeasurably more than all we ask or imagine, according to his power that is at work within us, 21 to him be glory in the church and in Christ Jesus throughout all generations, for ever and ever! Amen.*

Remember when I mentioned we'd requested two children on our paperwork, but we received only one referral? And we truly didn't understand why God did that? Why He shut that door? Why we'd knocked and knocked and knocked and He didn't open it? We'd asked and asked and asked. And He said no? This is a prime example of how He knows best.

What you'll go on to find out in the "Our Story" chapter, is that Chase and I both went into liver failure upon returning home. And my onset of liver failure- yeah, it was totally on the 14-hour leg of our 18-hour trip home. On the plane. Repeatedly throwing up. (Among other things.) Chase was able to take of our son and walk around the plane while I was busy being super sick.

So, have you truly pictured this? Me, throwing up all over my lap tray and repeatedly getting up and rushing to the restroom. Chase walking around the plane with our son. Now, imagine all that... with another child. A second child. That we'd only met for 3 weeks. Didn't your mind just go, ohhhhhhh..... I know! Not only was the plane ride horrible, but about three weeks later, we both ended up in the hospital for over a week. Keep reading if you want to find out the cause of our troubles. Then, within 4 months of being home, we found out we were expecting.

Now, it's with the ultimate peace and understanding that it completely makes sense why we didn't receive two children with our first adoption. Things would have been chaos. It wouldn't have been for the best for our children or for us, or for our daughter that would arrive 12 months later.

So, mommas, don't be discouraged when the mailbox is empty. Or, when you knock, and the door doesn't open. Trust in Him. Know that HE IS DOING more than you could even think to ask for. He is doing BIG things. And it's going to be beautiful. Enjoy the ride momma. You're going to have so many amazing stories. So many moments where your mind is going to be blown with His goodness. His power. His foresight. His provision. You're going to be blown away. And over and over again, He's going to show you... He loves you. And, He's got this.

MY LETTER TO ME

Thanks Brad Paisley.

Have you ever listened to that song? "A Letter to Me"? It's a song about how Brad - yeah, we're on a first name basis- sike, I wish- if he could, would go back in time and tell himself all the things he's learned over the years. It's a pretty novel idea. So, I got to thinking, what if I wrote a letter to me? To my pre-adoptive self? I think it'd go something like this:

Kelley,

These next few years are going to last much longer than you ever thought. Instead of 9 months, it'll be more like 3 years. But, it's going to be okay. Crazy things is, for the first year of your adoption, you'll be praying for your son before he's ever born.

One of the best things you'll do over the next few years is plug into your church. Those people are going to become a lifeline for your family. They'll mean more to you that you'll ever imagine. They will walk with you each step of the journey. They'll help you raise support. They'll help you get your paperwork done. They'll be your support system. And, they'll be there in the airport when you come home. It'll be their picture with you in the airport that fills the walls of your nursery.

Once you announce your adoption, a lot of people will want to talk to you. They'll open up and share their stories with you. You'll find out that a surprising number of your friends are adopted and were just waiting to have someone who'd connect with them, to share that detail. You'll have a lot of conversations about the need for adoption. And, you'll have a lot of people that think adoption is a good idea, but is just too hard or is not for them. You'll especially run into a lot of people that think you're making a mistake for adopting internationally instead of domestic. Now is the time to dig deep into scripture. Know why you're doing what you're doing. Plan ahead for those conversations. Because, every conversation you have, is an opportunity to point people back to Jesus. So, spend the time now, learning what scripture says about adoption. That way, when they world tells you their thoughts about it, you'll be ready to tell them the Gospel's thoughts about adoption. And how beautiful it is. And when someone says something that hurts you, remember what your daddy always told you-you catch more flies with honey than vinegar.

There are going to be several different seasons in your adoption. Seasons where things go so stinking smoothly. And others, not so much. In those tough seasons, dig deep. Remember the heart of what you're doing- Because He adopted you. Remember that when it's so tough and you get discouraged, that this was Plan A for your life. In fact, long before you ever began considering adoption, God was ordaining things in your life just to prepare you for it. Things you had no idea would have anything to do with your adoption. Things that were tough to go through, but in the end provided the biggest relief because they weren't one more weight to carry around during your adoption. Allow God to purify your life. Be open, now, to change.

Go ahead and start looking for an adoption group. Whether it's online or in person. The people in those groups will be a huge asset to you. You're going to have a ton of questions. The paperwork can be kind of confusing. These people will be your saving grace. These are people you'll live the rest of your lives with, from afar. It's amazing the way God knits His plans for our lives together. There are people all over the country whose lives have been interwoven with yours, and you haven't even met them yet.

Speaking of paperwork, there's a lot of it, but it's totally doable. The best thing you can do now is make yourself an adoption file bucket and master spreadsheet. Get your documents listed out, when they're do, and when they need to be updated. Do the same thing with your fees. It'll save your sanity in the long-run to have this organized when you're looking for a specific document.

And always remember, you're not alone. While it may seem at times like you're an island, you're not. This was HIS idea. Adoption is His thing. He created it. Trust Him to carry you through. He stretched out the empty sky and hung the earth on nothing. Trust Him to move mountains. Trust Him to show up. He will. This WILL be the best season of your life. You are about to see God more clearly than you ever have. Your life will be radically changed. There will not be one praise song on the radio that won't turn your heart back to worship. You are going to experience God so clearly that you will be hard-pressed to find a moment in any conversation that won't naturally turn back to you talking about how God good is. Just wait.

Oh, and, keep a prayer journal just for your adoption. You'll be encouraged as you're writing your prayers down, to be able to read all the prayers He's already answered.

See you in 3 years,

Kelley.

HIS LETTER TO YOU

Scripture Go-To-Guide

All the hope you'll ever need to complete your adoption written down in the sweet words of the Gospel. Mommas, I made this chapter for you, thinking of all the times I'd grab my Bible and look for just the right scripture. You know, the one that hits the sweet spot. The one that has the exact words you need to hear at just that moment. And what's even better is there are a thousand more scriptures that you'll find in His Word that will give you hope, encouragement, and endurance for the journey ahead. These are just the ones that I frequently referred to.

Why we adopt:

➤ Galatians 4:4-7: *But when the set time had fully come, God sent his Son, born of a woman, born under the law, 5 to redeem those under the law, that we might receive adoption to sonship.[7] 6 Because you are his sons, God sent the Spirit of his Son into our hearts, the Spirit who calls out, "Abba,[c] Father." 7 So you are no longer a slave, but God's child; and since you are his child, God has made you also an heir.*

➤ James 1:27: *Religion that God our Father accepts as pure and faultless is this: to look after orphans and widows in their distress and to keep oneself from being polluted by the world.*

---

[7] Galatians 4:5 The Greek word for *adoption* to sonship is a legal term referring to the full legal standing of an adopted male heir in Roman culture.

➤ Psalm 82:3: *Defend the weak and the fatherless; uphold the cause of the poor and the oppressed.*

➤ Proverbs 31:8-9: *Speak up for those who cannot speak for themselves, for the rights of all who are destitute. Speak up and judge fairly; defend the rights of the poor and needy.*

God's heart for orphans:

➤ Deuteronomy 12:18: *He defends the cause of the fatherless and the widow, and loves the foreigner residing among you, giving them food and clothing. 19 And you are to love those who are foreigners, for you yourselves were foreigners in Egypt. 20 Fear the Lord your God and serve him. Hold fast to him and take your oaths in his name.*

➤ Hosea 14:3: *Assyria cannot save us; we will not mount warhorses; We will never again say 'Our gods' to what our own hands have made, for in you the fatherless find compassion."*

➤ Matthew 25:40: *"The King will reply, 'Truly I tell you, whatever you did for one of the least of these brothers and sisters of mine, you did for me.'*

➤ Psalm 146: 9: *The Lord watches over the foreigner and sustains the fatherless and the widow, but he frustrates the ways of the wicked.*

➤ Psalm 68:5-6: *A father to the fatherless, a defender of widows, is God in his holy dwelling. God sets the lonely in families.*

➤ Psalm 10:14-18: *But you, God, see the trouble of the afflicted; you consider their grief and take it in hand; The victims commit themselves to you; you are the helper of the fatherless .15 Break the arm of the wicked man; call the evildoer to account for his wickedness that would not otherwise be found out.16 The Lord is King for ever and ever; the nations will perish from his land.17 You, Lord, hear the desire of the afflicted; you encourage them, and you listen to their cry,18 defending the fatherless and the oppressed, so that mere earthly mortals will never again strike terror.*

God will come through. Every time.

➤   2 Samuel 22:

David sang to the Lord the words of this song when the Lord delivered him from the hand of all his enemies and from the hand of Saul. 2 He said:

"The Lord is my rock, my fortress and my deliverer;
3   my God is my rock, in whom I take refuge,
my shield[a] and the horn[b] of my salvation.
He is my stronghold, my refuge and my savior—
from violent people you save me.
4 "I called to the Lord, who is worthy of praise,
and have been saved from my enemies.
5 The waves of death swirled about me;
the torrents of destruction overwhelmed me.
6 The cords of the grave coiled around me;
the snares of death confronted me.
7 "In my distress I called to the Lord;
I called out to my God.
From his temple he heard my voice;
my cry came to his ears.
8 The earth trembled and quaked,
the foundations of the heavens[c] shook;
they trembled because he was angry.
9 Smoke rose from his nostrils;
consuming fire came from his mouth,
burning coals blazed out of it.
10 He parted the heavens and came down;
dark clouds were under his feet.
11 He mounted the cherubim and flew;

he soared[d] on the wings of the wind.
12 He made darkness his canopy around him—
the dark[e] rain clouds of the sky.
13 Out of the brightness of his presence
bolts of lightning blazed forth.
14 The Lord thundered from heaven;
the voice of the Most High resounded.
15 He shot his arrows and scattered the enemy,
with great bolts of lightning he routed them.
16 The valleys of the sea were exposed
and the foundations of the earth laid bare
at the rebuke of the Lord,
at the blast of breath from his nostrils.
17 "He reached down from on high and took hold
of me;
he drew me out of deep waters.
18 He rescued me from my powerful enemy,
from my foes, who were too strong for me.
19 They confronted me in the day of my disaster,
but the Lord was my support.
20 He brought me out into a spacious place;
he rescued me because he delighted in me.
21 "The Lord has dealt with me according to my
righteousness;
according to the cleanness of my hands he has
rewarded me.
22 For I have kept the ways of the Lord;
I am not guilty of turning from my God.
23 All his laws are before me;
I have not turned away from his decrees.
24 I have been blameless before him
and have kept myself from sin.
25 The Lord has rewarded me according to my
righteousness,
according to my cleanness[f] in his sight.
26 "To the faithful you show yourself faithful,
to the blameless you show yourself blameless,

*27 to the pure you show yourself pure,
but to the devious you show yourself shrewd.
28 You save the humble,
but your eyes are on the haughty to bring them low.
29 You, Lord, are my lamp;
the Lord turns my darkness into light.
30 With your help I can advance against a troop[g];
with my God I can scale a wall.
31 "As for God, his way is perfect:
The Lord's word is flawless;
he shields all who take refuge in him.
32 For who is God besides the Lord?
And who is the Rock except our God?
33 It is God who arms me with strength[h]
and keeps my way secure.
34 He makes my feet like the feet of a deer;
he causes me to stand on the heights.
35 He trains my hands for battle;
my arms can bend a bow of bronze.
36 You make your saving help my shield;
your help has made[i] me great.
37 You provide a broad path for my feet,
so that my ankles do not give way.
38 "I pursued my enemies and crushed them;
I did not turn back till they were destroyed.
39 I crushed them completely, and they could not
rise;
they fell beneath my feet.
40 You armed me with strength for battle;
you humbled my adversaries before me.
41 You made my enemies turn their backs in flight,
and I destroyed my foes.
42 They cried for help, but there was no one to save
them—
to the Lord, but he did not answer.
43 I beat them as fine as the dust of the earth;
I pounded and trampled them like mud in the
streets.*

44 "You have delivered me from the attacks of the peoples;
you have preserved me as the head of nations.
People I did not know now serve me,
45   foreigners cower before me;
as soon as they hear of me, they obey me.
46 They all lose heart;
they come trembling[j] from their strongholds.
47 "The Lord lives! Praise be to my Rock!
Exalted be my God, the Rock, my Savior!
48 He is the God who avenges me,
who puts the nations under me,
49   who sets me free from my enemies.
You exalted me above my foes;
from a violent man you rescued me.
50 Therefore I will praise you, Lord, among the nations;
I will sing the praises of your name.
51 "He gives his king great victories;
he shows unfailing kindness to his anointed,
to David and his descendants forever."

The power of God; He is able:

➢ 2 Chronicles 20:6: *Lord, the God of our ancestors, are you not the God who is in heaven? You rule over all the kingdoms of the nations. Power and might are in your hand, and no one can withstand you.*

➢ Job 26: 7-14: *He spreads out the northern skies over empty space; he suspends the earth over nothing.8 He wraps up the waters in his clouds, yet the clouds do not burst under their weight. He covers the face of the full moon, spreading his clouds over it.10 He marks out the horizon on the face of the waters for a boundary between light and darkness. 11 The pillars of the heavens quake, aghast at his rebuke. 12 By his power he churned up the sea; by his wisdom he cut Rahab to pieces.13 By his breath the skies became fair; his hand pierced the gliding serpent.14 And these are but the outer fringe of his works; how faint the whisper we hear of him! Who then can understand the thunder of his power?*

Did you catch that last one? It's the main scripture I prayed over and over and over. He *spreads out the northern skies over empty space; he suspends the earth over nothing.* That verse. It was my hope. It was my stronghold. There is nothing He can't do. He literally hangs the earth on nothing. I mean. Who can do that? How is that possible? But, we know it's true, don't we? We've studied it in school. We've made models of the solar system. We know the earth- and all the planets- are literally suspended on nothing. And, it's recorded right there in scripture.

So, when I became discouraged. When the paperwork was just too much. When the wait was just too long. I prayed that scripture. "God, you are the God who stretches out the northern skies. You hung the earth on nothing. There is nothing you can't do. So, please, with your power, show up big in our adoption. Do something so big here that when people hear our story, they can't not believe in you."

Mommas, there's nothing He can't do.

SPOONFUL OF SUGAR

When God debunks adoption myths.

If your family is just now considering adoption, this is the perfect place to start. When you're poised with such a big task- like adoption, it can be daunting. The thought of having to raise thousands of dollars can be more than just a little overwhelming. So, if that's you, if you're in a place of *Could we really do this? Is God calling us to adoption?* Read on! See just how marvelously God provides when we are obedient to His Will and say Yes to hard things.

I've given you tons of tips and insight into the heart of adoption. Things that can go wrong. Things that go well. And ways to make things better. I'm going to leave you with a list of sorts that I think will put a big ole' smile on your face. Consider me your very own Mary Poppins. I'm going to give you a good ole' dose of hope and encouragement. A spoonful of sugar is just what you'll need to sing your way through this journey.

I'm going to list all the unsettling things people say about adoption and how God punches them in the face.

1. **Adoption is too expensive. It's not possible.** Our adoption goal was $30,000. We had a debt free adoption. Oh yes. We raised every stinking dime.

   a. **Yard sales are lousy fundraisers:** Our first yard sale: $900. Our second yard sale: $1,400.

   b. **You have to be super rich to adopt:** The year before we started the adoption process, our combined income was around $40,000. We were tasked with raising ¾ of one year's worth of income to adopt. It happened.

2. **People won't give to adoptions:**

   a. A friend told her doctor our story and he cut us a check for $400 without knowing us.

   b. A lady in my small group used her tax return to pay for our home study instead of buying a van. Our home study cost $1,400. She said something to this effect, "We can't adopt right now, but we can bring your children home."

   c. Some friends that lived in the apartment above us when we first moved to NC paid for one of our plane tickets in full. Did I mention this was two years after we moved out of that complex? They hadn't seen us, but maybe once, over the course of those years, yet sent us a Facebook message asking for the cost of our flights because they wanted to buy one of our tickets.

   d. One day at church a family gave us all of their name-brand baby gear. A rock-n-play. A Chicco stroller. A bumbo with tray.

   e. A co-worker gave me a Britax car seat and TWO bases. CaChing!

   f. Another friend gave us a crib in amazing condition.

   g. A couple we went to church with donated over $2,000 worth in venue and horderves for our adoption gala.

h. A baker donated a gorgeous huge cake for our gala.

i. Bonefish grill donated a free 4-course menu sampling for a party of eight for our silent auction at the gala.

j. Another adopting couple gave us $800 to help us meet our first big goal, all the while fundraising for their own adoption.

k. A concert venue downtown donated the use of their facility, so we could have an adoption concert.

l. For the concert, a well-known band donated their time as their gift to our adoption. How did this come about? The lead singer's mom just so happened to be a substitute at the school where I taught. I asked her what she thought about it. Then, booked the band!

m. A guy we went to church with saw their neighbor put their swing set up for sale. For free. Our friend took the day off of work to go disassemble the play set and then come over to our house, assemble it, and power wash it, with the help of two other great friends, all to surprise us when we got home from work. He said, "Thought your kids might need this." I know! Crazy. #God

n. A pastor at our church bought $200 worth of gala tickets to giveaway for the first 8 people to come and ask for them.

o. A guy I worked with played on a recreational soccer team. He had his whole team buy our shirts and wear them as their team shirts. They were the "Love. Redemption. Adoption." team.

    i.   Let's take a moment here just to think about what that means. Between 10-20 men are walking around NC wearing adoption shirts. Think about those conversation starters! Bam.

p.   This one blows my mind: The largest single donor of our adoption (outside of the airline tickets and gala venue donation) was a young widowed mom of four, who was in the middle of starting her own business. Every few weeks, we'd receive a check for a few hundred dollars from her. In total, we received over $1,000 from her alone. While we were taking care of orphans, God used this beautiful widow to take care of us.

3. **The paperwork is too hard.**

a.   Our bank and my doctor filled out our home study paperwork for free- twice.

b.   In applying for PAIR Approval with our referral, we hadn't heard anything for a few weeks after sending it in. I called. The gentlemen on the phone said it could be weeks before the officer assigned to our case even looked at it. We had everyone praying. When I arrived home that afternoon, the PAIR packet was sitting in my mailbox. Meaning- not only had it been picked up off of our officer's desk, but it had been picked up, processed, and sent back to us!

    c. Our son's paperwork was done in 3 days in Ethiopia. That was the fastest our attorney said he'd ever seen it happen in 10 years.

4. Adoption is an island. There's no support.

    a. Our friend paid for our home study.

    b. Our neighbor paid for our flight.

    c. Every inch of our son's nursery was outfitted by the generosity of others. And, we're not talking just gently used stuff, we're talking brand-new, and name brand!

    d. Friends and family threw us FOUR baby showers.

    e. There were over 30 people in the airport waiting for us to come home.

    f. We had meals for over three weeks provided by friends and family.

    g. We do a gift card exchange every year for Christmas at work. The year we were adopting, instead of trading cards, they gave them all to me. They were all Babies R US gift cards.

    h. Our notary was a friend from church. She met me at all sorts of weird and inconvenient hours to help get our paperwork squared away. I'm pretty sure she could have bought a car with all the times we needed her notary if she charged per seal! Yet, she did it free of charge. Every. Single. Time.

i. A friend met us at our house at 2 in the morning and drove us to the airport over an hour away.

j. We flew to Ethiopia August 8th. School started later that month. My long-term substitute and team handled all of the plans. I didn't have to write one lesson plan.

k. Other adoptive families provided forms and boat-loads of advice throughout the entire process and often at the wee hours in the morning. When I tried to get addresses to send thank you cards, they refused. They just wanted to help.

5. **Adoption is only for the young.**

   a. Now, obviously we did start this adoption young. We were 24 and 25 when we applied to our agency. So, this old adage doesn't quite apply to us, but we were told time and again, "If I was younger, I'd adopt." Well, let me stop you right there. In Ethiopia, we met this amazing amazing woman. She was fifty. Single. And on her second adoption. Y'all. She legitimately could have been my mom. And here she was, adopting. We had court on the same day. We both became moms on the same day. Even though we were 25 years apart, we were starting fresh with a new-to-us bundle of joy. It can be done! When I grow up, I want to be like her. At one point during our stay in Ethiopia, Chase got super sick and so did our son. What did I do? Went and hung out with her. When I was missing a form I had no idea we'd need for the lawyer, guess who had an extra copy? She did! That's the beauty of adopting a little later in life. You've got your stuff together. It's the perfect time to adopt! When we got home and I couldn't get our son to eat anything from a spoon because he wanted to feed himself, who did I call? Her!!! Keep in mind, the Lord often asks us to do things that seem crazy to us, but in His Plan- Plan A- they make perfect sense.

i. Think about Abraham and Sarah. Why is this story so popular? Cause it's crazy. He was a hundred. She was ninety. And she birthed Isaac. If you're out of your "child bearing" years and are somewhere around the "empty nester" stage, but feel a call to adopt, foster, or take care of vulnerable children in any capacity, remember Abraham and Sarah. Be obedient. Don't get hung up on a number. Don't make plans to spend the rest of your days on the earth reminiscing on the glory days. Instead, plan to fill your days with His glory. 2 Peter 3:8-9 tells us, "But do not let this one fact escape your notice, beloved, that with the Lord one day is like a thousand years, and a thousand years like one day."

As you can see, time and time again, God is in the details. You know that old adage, "Go big or go home"?

Pretty sure God coined that phrase. Don't let anyone tell you it can't be done. He'll do it. Every time. He always shows up.

I told my friends often, if you want to see God move mountains, adopt! One phrase we prayed over and over that was that God would do something so big that when anyone looked at our story (of adoption) that they couldn't deny God exists. If you look back at that list, I think you can see He answered that prayer. BIG TIME.

OUR STORY

All the good feels.

By this point, you've probably realized our story didn't start because we couldn't get pregnant. It started a little differently. My husband and I had traveled to Anderson, SC to support our little sister at a choral performance at Anderson University. Fabulous school by the way! While there, Chase had set-up a few meetings with people from the church he'd interned with while in college. A lot of these people had become financial supporters of Chase and I when we moved to help launch a church in NC. In one of these meetings to catch up, Chase had a really interesting conversation. The guy said, "What could you do with $25,000 dollars?"

Chase posed that question to me as we passed the Jockey Lot on the way home. My immediate response was, "We could adopt a kid with that."

See- I'd already looked all this up. A year or so before this conversation, I worked at the YMCA Kids Camp during the summer while school was out. I fell in love with a little boy, only to later find out that he was in foster care. We went on to approach the conversation of adoption through a friend-of-a-friend. Eventually, we were talking to the foster parents and they were rooting for us. The social worker, however, not so much. We had an extremely hard time getting her on the phone, agreeing to meet with us, even just having a nice conversation was a struggle. Over and over, our persistence was ignored and even perceived as annoying. It eventually became clear that she was not going to be an advocate for us in the adoption of this sweet little boy.

Soap Box Moment- This was a learning moment for us. A crazy hard one. Why on earth would we- two young loving people with a steady income- be turned down, let alone basically not even be considered- as potential adoptive parents of a little boy who has no other adoptive parent candidates and is in desperate need of adoption?

The only way I can now understand this is with the hindsight that that sweet little boy is now in a forever home that is perfect for him. A home perfectly suited for him where all the attention will be doted on him. A home, that now is completely opposite of ours, as we were just beginning to grow our family. A home, in which, would in the long run, have offered a lot less attention focused solely on him. This is a concept I understand now, nearly 6 years later. This is a prime example of when we knock and knock and knock and God doesn't open the door. It's because He gives the BEST to His children. We would have never been the BEST for that sweet little boy.

What this experience did offer me, however, was a way to shut people up. Perhaps that doesn't seem super nice, but it is a part of our story. When we were asked, "Why don't you adopt here from the US? Don't OUR kids matter?" I was able to legitimately say, we tried, and that door was slammed shut. It also made us ready for the moment we got offered $25,000. Since we'd been turned down to adopt from foster care, I'd started looking into other avenues for taking care of vulnerable children- like international adoption.

Moving on. Chase looked at me like, "For real, you wanna adopt a kid? You don't want to pay off debt or something?" My response was something like "We'll - probably- always have debt, we won't always have the opportunity to adopt." With that, the ball began to roll.

We talked and spent a few weeks looking up countries to adopt from. What it came down to for us were basic requirements for each country. Because of my age, at the time I was 24, we didn't meet the age requirements of most countries for adoptive parents. That boiled us down to Ethiopia and Bulgaria. At the time, the youngest a child could be adopted from Bulgaria was 5 years old. Bearing in mind the experience we had with trying to adopt an older child in foster care, we felt it best to move in the direction of Ethiopia, a country who placed children available for adoption at 3 months of age.

Upon agreeing on a country, we needed to find an adoption placing agency. We scoured the internet and then sought counsel with friends who were adoptive parents. Upon deciding on an agency, we sent our application and the application fee. Our first check. $300.

We were accepted into the Ethiopian Adoption Program. The next step was to find a local agency to complete our home study- our placing agency was on the other side of the country. When we found an agency, we kind of hit a dead spot. You see, with this agency, an international home study was $1,400. The money from the donor that wanted to offer $25,000 hadn't come in. We'd just bought our first home the summer of 2012. We'd used pretty much all of our funds for the down payment. There wasn't an extra $1,400 laying around.

We found ourselves trying to walk the line of being nice, not pushy, but direct with the donor in trying to get the money. We waited three months and contacted him during those months. Eventually, we found out, through no fault of the donor, the money he had generously planned to gift to our family, had become tied up in legal hemispheres and would be delivered at no certain time. So, we realized, it's time. Let's pull ourselves up by our bootstraps and get this $1,400 raised.

And, we were still at a standstill. I was working. Chase was working. Literally, no light bulbs went off as to how we were going to come up with that money. I shared our concern about the money and the call we felt had been clearly placed on our hearts to adopt with the women's small-group that was meeting at my house at the time. A week later, one of the ladies came up to me with a check for $1,400 and said, "We can't adopt right now, but we can help bring your kids home."

Can we stop for a minute and just say, "Holy cow?!?" That was a huge chunk of their tax return. The very tax return they had planned on using to help them buy a van to carry their own 4 children around in. They CHOSE NOT TO GET A VAN AND INSTEAD TO BRING OUR KIDS HOME.

If you've been discouraged in your journey, reread that last paragraph. God cares. HE shows up. And it can happen in the most unusual and unexpected ways.

Needless to say, we cashed that check, applied to the home study agency and worked on our home study. The home study- as you know- required lots of papers to be submitted before we could even meet with the social worker. Things like bank declarations, doctor's appointments, physicals, reference letters, employment letters. All that stuff. Can you say, wooh?

Well, lucky for us, in this aspect of my life, I'm pretty Type A. So, with reluctance on my husband's end, I sent him to a see a doctor for the very first time since moving to NC. A lady doctor at that. So, you can imagine his dismay when he realized she expected him to have a true physical. I legitimately do not remember the last time I laughed as hard as I did when I got a text a work that explained what happened at his appointment. Oh boy, oh boy.

The doctor's paperwork ended up being a breeze, along with employment letters. The bank letters, not so much. Insert super frustrated emoji here. I went to the bank. The guy was super nice and wrote exactly the letter we needed. I went out to the center of the bank to have the receptionist notarize it. You know- because you basically end up with your forehead being notarized because no paper is official without it having a notary's seal. Well, the girl at the bank screwed up the notary. She looked at me and said, "You think they'll mind if I scribble this out and put my initials on it?" My response was, "This paper is going to Africa, I can't take a chance of having a scribble." She looked at me. She looked back at the bank manager guy's door, which was now closed, and went on to inform me that unfortunately he'd be tied up in meetings the rest of the day and she could not interrupt. Perfect. P-uuuur-feccct.

So, I took my messed-up bank declaration and headed to another branch to see if they'd fix the paper for me, aka- redo it from scratch. Well, this new bank lady looked at me as if I was a dragon with five heads in her room that was asking her to serve me dinner and wine. Legitimately. She looked at me as if I'd lost my mind. So, I re-explained to her what just happened and what I needed to be typed up. Her response: "What kind of paperwork did you have to show him you are adopting. You need paperwork for this kind of letter. I can't believe he did this for you. I need proof. If this is for real, you must have some type of paperwork PROVING you're adopting."

So, at that point I started crying. I looked at her, and in my not-so-finest-moment, said, "Really, just forget-it, you're just one more person who doesn't care."

Y'all, all I needed was a statement on bank letterhead of how long our account had been open, how much was in our account, and that we were in good standing.

She responded, "Of course I care. I mean. It's great what you're doing for the babies. But I can't do that without proof."

I stood. Thanked her for her time. And left. Completely defeated.

You see mommas, you may have confidence in what you're doing. But, to put it simply, everyone won't care. Everyone won't jump to help you. A lot of people will still choose to focus on the complexities of their 9-5 job and how you're an inconvenience to them, instead of how a few minutes of time can help save vulnerable children.

I told my husband my saga over bang bang shrimp at Bonefish Grill. Remember mommas- we are going to experience things as emotional losses. We are geared that way. Our husbands are likely to look at what we see as emotional losses as simply annoying obstacles. Chase's response was, "Well, let me do it." And he did. He went to another branch location. Got the paper filled out. And his paper came with a smiling receptionist who was more than happy to help.

With our papers filled out and submitted to our home study agency, it was time to start working toward our next financial goal. It was around $3,750 and we would send it to our placing agency. So, it was time to throw a yard sale.

We threw a killer yard sale thanks to the help of friends and family. We had lots of people drop off their gently used extras and stored them for several weeks. Our garage was a madhouse to say the least. When the time came for the garage sale, we ended up needing the church's 24ft U-Haul to load everything up and take it to our yard sale spot. A couple, friends of ours, had offered to let us use their yard since it was in the center of a busy part of the city. At that yard sale, we grossed over $900. Can you say holy cow? No. Okay. I'll say it for you. HOLY COW. #Hedidthat!

To top that all off, upon leaving the yard sale, we got a call from friends of ours who were literally in the process of adopting two of their own children from Ethiopia, using the same agency as us, and were currently fundraising too. Ya know what they said? They asked us how much we needed to meet our next goal. We said about $800. They put a check in the mail that day for us. Even though they were raising for their own adoption. Did you get that? Isn't that crazy? Now, hold on to your seat. Would you believe they let us know that within the next week someone randomly reimbursed them that entire amount without even knowing they'd given that much money to us? It's God folks. This is HIS business. Trust Him to do what HE does best!

Between the yard sale, donations on our website, and the financial gift from our friends, we were able to send off that first BIG payment. After that, we needed to work on our first round of BIG paperwork that was going to USCIS and complete the home study requirements. We were able to get those things sent off and approved within two months. I will add here, that part of this process was having the papers sent back to us, having to re-do a few of them, and resubmit them. So, don't get discouraged if everything doesn't go super smoothly. They rarely do, but that's ok. You'd rather have small things to fix earlier on, rather than have them delay your child coming home later down the road.

Once we received that approval, we were ready to send everything in with our dossier, except for the payment. This was an even bigger payment of over $12,000. We continued to sell puzzle pieces online, t-shirts, and receive profits from justlovecoffee.com.

Here's a cool story from this season of fundraising: A guy I taught with played on a rec-league soccer team. He had all of them buy our shirts. THE WHOLE TEAM. And that was their team shirt. That they wore to every game. Isn't that insane? I didn't even know he was on a team.

One day after work, a group of us teachers went out for appetizers. I shared our story. He said, "I think I could get my guys to buy your shirts." I showed up the next week at their field and every gentleman handed me $20 and said "keep the change." We walked away with over $200 that night. Stop it!!! Is this real life?!? Yes. #OnlyGod

While those profits were great, we weren't making huge strides towards our goal. So, we got creative.

With the help of some amazing friends, we threw an adoption gala. Our dear friends paid for the use of renting out their country club for a day and paid for catering. This was a ticketed event with a buffet, dancing, silent auction, Ethiopian coffee bar, photo booth, fancy cake, and DJ. After a lot of mingling, we took the opportunity with tons of friends and family there to share our story, thank our friends and family for their involvement, and educate them on the importance of adoption.

Throughout the course of the night, we were able to continue to raise money through a few things:

• The silent auction had donations of everything from massages to child care.
• The Ethiopian Coffee bar had really nice packages made up of hand-roasted coffee beans that were for sale. (Thanks to an amazing friend who made all of these packages for us!)
• We had a wine ring toss. We set up wine bottles and for $5, you could stand back and try and toss 10 rings around the neck of a wine bottle. If you've ever been to a state or local fair, they've probably had this event with really large teddy bears or bags of gold fish as the prize. Surprisingly, even without the large teddy bears, this event was a HUGE success. I should note, this game is VERY hard. Few people won. But, everyone wanted to play. So, in the end, I totally recommend this. If you're not comfortable using bottles filled with wine, use empty

wine bottles and glue them down on a plastic washing machine tray.

• Kiosk set-up to allow people to donate as they felt moved.

With the GALA, we raised over $3,000. Never let the fear of the amount of your next payment stop you. We had several coffee dates leading up to this event where we shared our story with people. Crazy stories came out of those dates. Here's a short one- A lady came over for coffee and wanted to know why we were asking people to give us money to adopt, "Because you don't do that. People are responsible for raising and supporting their own families." Can you imagine how my heart sank when she told me that?

After coffee with her, she completely understood why we were adopting and why we were fundraising. She showed up to the gala with a $400 check from her doctor, whom she had shared our story with. WE'D NEVER MET THAT DOCTOR. But, she shared our story and he gave. THIS IS WHY YOU SHARE YOUR STORY. People want to get involved. People want to be generous. Give them the opportunity.

At the GALA, we even had someone propose to their girlfriend. It was awesome.

Here's a snapshot of the gala:

• People arrived. If they'd prepaid, their names were on the registry. If not, they paid at the door with cash or online at a kiosk we had set-up. (A friend let us use his iPad and we sat it on a stand.)

• People socialized while they moved around and made bids at the silent auction table, as well as visited the photo booth and other stations set-up around the room.

- Chase and I opened up the evening with a quick introduction and invited people to the buffet tables and announced when bidding would end.

- People ate. Live music played. One of our church's pastors played the music.

- Chase and I gave a compelling speech about adoption.

  - Why we were adopting.

  - Stats on adoption.

  - An invitation for them to adopt.

  - A thank you for their generosity and involvement in our adoption.   ·

  - Praise to God for what He was already doing.

- We announced winners of the silent auction.

- We ate cake.

- Dancing. A proposal. More dancing.

- One last "Thank you."

Something super cool that came out of all of the publicity for the gala was a friend from church- another momma- came to me and said she'd babysit our kids- for free- when we came home from Africa. Oh. My. Word. What a burden lifted. Because, childcare is something that'd been on our minds this whole time, too. We didn't want to just throw our kids back into a foster home setting- an environment with few adults and large amounts of children. We'd done a good bit of adoption education at this point and had learned that immediately rejoining that type of setting can be very traumatic for adopted children. So, her offer. An answered prayer.

By this point, we had enough to send off nearly $13,000. That was a crazy moment sitting in my car getting ready to send off that check. I went through a thousand thoughts. Here's my crazier ones:

- What if someone looks in the envelope and sees this huge check and steals it??

- What if it gets wet because it gets left out in the rain?

- What if they leave it by the door and someone takes it?

Moving on. By October, our dossier was in transit. Remember, everything has to have state and federal certification/notarization. And yes, we did have a few things that got sent back to us from NC because they didn't like the way a few forms were filled out. We corrected them, sent them back, and they were approved. Then, it was time to send the packet to our agency, who forwarded it onto DC. By November, it made it to Addis. By December 2013, we were officially a waiting family.

And in February of 2014, the laws of adoption began to change. Insert crying emoji here. Basically, they prolonged the waiting time until referral and decreased the waiting time post-referral. They had great reasons for doings this, I'm sure, but it didn't help this momma's heart at all.

Months would go by and we wouldn't hear ANYTHING from our agency. I'd check-in periodically and we were told to basically keep waiting. So, we did. We continued to fundraise with puzzle pieces and t-shirts. And wait. And wait. And wait.

One cool thing we did in the meantime was throw a concert. A venue downtown in our city hosted our event for free. We had a hit band come and play. We sold shirts. We made over $600 that night.

Another cool thing we did was make videos. I mentioned this in the fundraising portion of the book. In one video, we announced that our next fundraising goal of $14,000 included flights. Well, that same week, no lie, some friends, not even super close friends, sent us a Facebook message and said they wanted to buy one of our tickets! Hold the phone. That really happened. Want to know how they became our friends? They were our upstairs neighbors from the apartment complex we lived in two years prior to beginning the adoption. Y'all. This stuff doesn't happen in real life. #butGod.

And then we waited some more.

Until Dec. 4, 2014 when our whole world changed. Here's how it went:

It was a Thursday night and I was preparing my home for the ladies small group that was about to start. At this point, I'd become addicted to checking my email at any free moment. You know, just in case there was an email that said, "Referral." Low and behold, as ladies were walking in my door, an email from our agency popped up and said, "Happy Christmas: Referral."

I started FLIPPING OUT. Jumping. Screaming. Gosh, I'm even tearing up as I write this. We all lost it. Everyone was screaming and hugging each other. I saw the little paperclip on the email, so I knew there was a picture attached. But Chase, my husband, wasn't home. He was at church for band practice. ON THE COMPLETE OTHER SIDE OF TOWN. So, what did we do about small group? Well, we all loaded into the biggest car and drove to the other side of town. I called everyone possible on the way and of course... no one answered their phone. So stinking anti-climatic.

I got there. Ran inside. And with tears in my eyes told my sweet husband that we had THE email! So, we set up a table in the back of the sanctuary. Everyone that was there for band practice and from my small group gathered around and watched us as we locked eyes with our son for the very first time. That moment, folks, was like no other. I could never begin to explain to you the complexities of that moment.

The referral is packaged with all of the information they have about your child. Pictures. Birth certificate. How they came to be in the orphanage. For the briefest of moments there's joy. You have your child. You know their face. You know their name. And within seconds, it all comes crashing down because you realize- that's your child. In an orphanage. All alone. Without you. And then you read every gut-wrenching word of how your child came to be in the orphanage. I have never felt the depths of despair that I felt in that moment. The details here are for our family and our son only, but be prepared for this moment. Be reminded now that with the beauty of adoption for you, comes the most unfathomable loss and pain for your child. This will be a defining moment for you.

As I mentioned in the chapter "When the mailbox is empty", this was the moment we thought we received two children at referral, and instead only received one. While I won't repeat those events, I will reiterate the importance of community. The community that was there with us to celebrate the joy of our referral, was the same community that surrounded us as we grieved the loss of our second child and accepted that our adoption was going to look much different than we'd planned. Community y'all. You're going to need it.

We celebrated the referral of our son with the typical festivities associated with biological children. We had a gender reveal party where all of our family met-up in the closest city and opened an Oreo filled with blue icing.

Try hard not to overlook these moments. Your friends and family have journeyed with you. They want to celebrate too. They can't be there with you for ultrasound scans and feel your belly grow. But this, cutting a cake or hitting a piñata and waiting to see if pink or blue falls out of a balloon, that they can do. That, they want to do. So, do it. Celebrate. Your child is coming home, which means their niece/nephew/cousin/friend/child they've prayed for is coming home, too.

Once we accepted our referral, our son was moved from the orphanage, to the foster home. $400 a month. Best money we've ever spent. Happiest checks we've ever written.

Side note- Foster care in international countries doesn't always look like it does in America. For us, it looked like our son being moved to another orphanage. This orphanage was intended solely for kids who had adoptive parents lined up. So, these were kids that were in the process of being adopted. That was super helpful information to know. That way, when we got to visit him, we didn't feel as if we were neglecting the other children who were there, since they had parents coming for them, too.

After the referral email from our agency, we had to wait for a physical package to arrive. I referenced this part of our story in the chapter "When the mailbox is empty" about not knowing what the referral package would like. It came about three weeks later. We reviewed it. Signed every paper. And then, sent it off to USCIS beginning of January 2015. I emailed 3 weeks later just to check on the status of our paperwork. That was January 21st. On the 23rd, I received and email saying it had been received and would be WEEKS until it was assigned to an officer and reviewed.

Y'all. I can't make this up. I got home. That same day. Checked the mail. Like, the actual mailbox. IN THOSE THREE WEEKS, IT HAD NOT ONLY BEEN ASSIGNED TO AN OFFICER AND REVIEWED BUT PROCESSED AND SENT TO US!

We did have some things we had to resolve. And when I say resolve, I mean get stuff done by their deadline. Keep in mind here, this is when the United States was looking over the paperwork that Ethiopia had prepared and our dossier. We had until April 15 to get everything resolved.

The only thing about this step is that your USCIS officer isn't supposed to tell you anything. Like-answer any questions about the things they're telling you to fix. Why, you ask? Well, it's to guarantee people can't falsify documents. That's where it can get super tricky. You have to rely on your agency and people who have adopted before to help you figure this stuff out. Some of the things we had to fix- like our home study- were documents that were expiring.

We had no idea those things could even do that. Expire? Say what? That's one of those things that you learn by experience. So, we immediately called our home study agency and requested an expedited update. For an extra fee, of course, we were able to get that done. Then, it became a waiting game.

The best part of these months post-referral, was that we received weekly updates and photos of our son. You better believe that on Thursdays I never left my computer! Everyone at school knew Thursdays were picture days!

During this phase of time, we were simply waiting for PAIR Approval and 1 of 2 court dates that were to come.

That summer, I was taking a course at UNCG for teachers that were going to have interns in the fall. During that workshop, I got THE email that said we had a court date for July 10th and that thankfully, we received PAIR Approval, meaning all of the documents we had to fix in January were good to go. Wooh. Talk about a celebration. I went outside and called everybody. I mean. EVERYBODY. COURT DATE HERE WE COME! We wouldn't attend for this date, but we knew it was a significant date where the officer on our case would appear and attest that- yes, our son was eligible for adoption and that his paperwork was correct.

I returned to the class and told our instructor our big news. I ended up going up in front of everyone and sharing our son's picture and our story with a room of around 75 people!

Always. Always. Always share God's goodness. Your adoption story is a reminder of His love for us.

When I got home that day, the official letter of approval and court date was waiting in the mailbox. We cried and cried and cried. That was our last step of approval on the US side (kind of.) It was the last BIG hurdle to say the least.

Then, we had the most anti-climactic day ever. July 10th came and went. We never heard anything. Text after text came in from loving friends and family excited to hear how court went. I sat in the swing set late that evening and wept. I couldn't believe we didn't hear anything. We knew that after that court date, the next step was for us to get on a plane and go get our son. We also knew that Ethiopia was going to shut down for the rainy season sometime in August and not re-open until mid-October. So, the silence was deafening. If we didn't get the adoptive parent court date before the rainy season, it was going to be after October before it was even possible.

We found out later that the officer who was supposed to appear on our son's behalf July 10th never did and they couldn't locate him.

We continued to wait and with each passing day, we lost hope that we would see our son before the rainy season. So, we carried on as normal. After all, what else could we do? Toward the end of the summer, I went home to SC to help my parents get their house ready to sell and put on the market. While I was standing on top of the bathroom counter getting ready to tape the walls with painter's tape, my phone started ringing. I hopped down and grabbed it. As soon as I saw the Portland, OR area code, I FLIPPED OUT! I knew EXACTLY what that meant!!!! Here's how this conversation went:

(Agent) Hello, Kelley?

(Me) Yes.

(Agent) Hi. Yes. We have your court date. Can you be in Ethiopia by tomorrow at 2:15.

(Me) Is that even physically possible? It's an 18-hour flight and it's 1:00 pm now.

(Agent) I don't know. That's why I'm calling you. Call my travel agent and see what you can do.

So, I hung up. Walked into my parents' kitchen and we all freaked out! Cried. Hugged. And then, forgetting to call my husband, immediately called Adoption Airfare. If you haven't lined them up, even if you're doing domestic travel, USE THEM. They tried everything for us. Could they fly us out of Dallas, out of Florida, or even out of New York? They tried everywhere and everything to get us there by the next day.

I hung up with them while they tried to figure it out and called Chase. He was sitting in his barber's chair when he got the call. I told him, "So, we're going to Africa.

We've got court tomorrow." Can you imagine that conversation? Holy Cow. It was amazing. We'd waited 3 years to share that with each other. So, obviously, he had to tell his barber what was going on and decide whether or not there was time to finish his haircut!

I got back on the phone with Adoption Airfare and we conceded that it was not possible for us to make it on time. However, I thought- God's big, right? This is surely His kind of thing. Well, His word says all I need is faith as small as a mustard seed and He'll move mountains. So, I said a prayer. And told Adoption Airfare to book the next flight, we were going to Africa anyway and trusting that God would make a way.

Some might call that stupid. I call that having a glimpse of how BIG God is. Remember we prayed that God would do something so big in our adoption that when others heard our story, they'd have to believe? This was that moment. Something big was happening.

Obviously, I had to call our adoption agency back and tell them that- no, we can't make it by Friday at 2:15, but I may have already booked flights and we were trusting God that He'd do something big and the judge would see us. Y'all. He laughed at me. Turns out, our adoption agent was a Christian. Who knew? #Goddid

Oh. And the beauty of that phone call. I was wearing an #everychildmatters t-shirt that I had purchased to support a fund to help our son's foster home be able to purchase a drying machine. I just love that when I look back at pictures of that moment, my shirt says, "Every Child Matters." #littlethingsmakeyourstory

So, we called everyone. I drove home. We borrowed some luggage. We packed our house- basically- because who knows what you're going to need in a different county when you become a parent at the drop of a hat? So, everything. We packed. Everything.

At 2am on a Saturday morning, our friend dropped us off in Charlotte, NC and we went to meet our son. It doesn't get better than that!

We arrived in Addis around 7 am on a Sunday. Here's a detail that's important: know the address of where you're going. We had no idea. We knew the name of our son's foster home, but not the address. We knew the name of the guest house adoptive families stayed in, but not the address. We had an itinerary of what we would need to do and how much it would cost, but no address for anything! That was a HUGE and TERRIFYING hassle. Part of them approving your visa is telling them exactly where you're going. The language barrier didn't help either. They brought several guards in to try and figure out where we were going. Eventually, we got through.

Now, you may be thinking, *come on, how did you not know you needed an address for your visa?* Well, here's how: we found out on a Thursday we were headed to Africa and landed three days later. There was no time. It didn't dawn on us to think, *Hey, we should send an email and get the exact address of the guest house.*

We walked through to luggage claim. Got our stuff. And then realized, we have no clue what to do from this point forward. We looked around and a lot of the taxi drivers kept saying, "You American? You go with me?" I looked at Chase. He looked at me. We said, "I don't know." We continued to walk around and finally came to our driver who had a sign with "Lambert Family" and our son's name on it. Talk about stress relief. This is when I'd like to go back in time and remind myself that God is in the details. There's no need to worry about things even as small as who your taxi driver is going to be.

Our driver took us to the hotel we'd be staying in and told us he'd be back in two hours to take us to visit our son for the very first time.

Then, the time came. It was pouring rain on that Sunday when we met our son for the very first time. And for the first time in our adoption journey, I didn't lose it. I didn't flip out. I didn't cry. I looked at my son. And I gained the whole world.

The days repeated with us allowed to visit him for two hours at a time, twice a day until Wednesday, when we had court.

We met our Ethiopian attorney that day- as in- we shook his hand for the first time in the car on the way to court. On the ride to the courthouse, he briefed us on what would happen. What we would be asked and what things would mean. We were among 4 families having court that day. Each family had their turn going in and coming out. When it was our turn, it was just us, the judge, and our attorney. He asked very standard questions and the one I'll never forget is this:

- You understand this is a fact, yes? This cannot be undone.

And I nodded my head as fast as it would go- picture a bobblehead on a car dash- that was me!

We left the courthouse and went to our lawyer's office. We paid fees and were told there were more forms to fill-out. We had no idea. Make sure you know there's always going to be another form required. Have extra of every form on hand. By the grace of God, another lady adopting with us brought multiple copies and let us use some of her forms!

Another important note here is to bring large and small bills. We needed a $5 bill. The lawyer had no change and would not allow extra money/keep the change. We ended up walking out of his office and asking all the other families adopting with us if we could have 5 bucks! God knew we would run into this dilemma and another couple there handed us the cash.

Then, we went to the foster home and signed our son out! Literally. There was a form. We signed him out. Permanently. Best. Feeling. Ever. There are a lot of pictures from our time in Ethiopia, but I believe the picture of him in my arms while I sign that document is my absolute favorite.

There were several paperwork things that had to be taken care of during this time as well. We had to get the court paperwork approved, hard copies of his birth certificate, and a passport made for him. It was a lot. However, it was all done by that Friday. Let me say that again.

- We arrived on Sunday.
- Had court on Wednesday.
- Paperwork done by Friday.

Our attorney said that was the fastest turn around he'd ever seen on paperwork and he'd been doing it for 10 years. - This is where you say- #God

From there, we lived the next two and a half weeks in the hotel. We figured out feeding, napping, changing diapers, and bath-time all in one fell-swoop. Talk about a whirlwind. During this time, our son had projectile vomit and diarrhea. Can you imagine being first-time parents, in a foreign country, with no family nearby, and your child is pooping and vomiting EVERYWHERE? It was INSANE. I still remember being on my hands and knees using a bar of soap to scrub the poop stains out of the carpet of the hotel.

Those weeks were challenging, but they were fun. So very, very fun. We got to live in community with the other families adopting, which was amazing! We are all still in touch and will never forget the sweet time we shared together in Ethiopia. We walked around and explored our son's birth country. We visited missionaries that the other adoptive families knew of. We toured Embracing Hope

Ethiopia's facilities- an amazing agency that helps vulnerable families stay together by providing childcare so single mothers can work and earn a livable wage, to prevent them from having to orphan their children. We ate in local restaurants. We went to the market and bought tons of souvenirs. We did a lot. We also face-timed a lot. We kept in touch with friends and family by using Facebook messenger. The hotel we stayed in, thankfully, had internet. We were able to facetime and message our families without extreme rates or using our data! Again, God is in the details!

A good memory I have from this in-between time is taking trips to a local coffee shop, Kaldi's. It's pretty similar to Starbucks. If you're ever in Africa, go! It's AMAZING!! We'd been sitting down and enjoying our coffee for a good 30 minutes. Next thing we knew, our son threw-up everywhere. I was so embarrassed. We tried to discreetly clean everything up before anyone noticed.

On our way home from one of our trips to Kaldi's, it poured rain. Like, you've never seen so much in your life. It was CRAZY. Hail. Y'all. Hail came down. In a matter of minutes, it went from sunny skies- skies so beautiful we thought it was the perfect time to walk several blocks to Kaldi's- to flooding rain and hail. It was UNREAL. Good times. We ended up huddled under a bus port with other Ethiopians as we waited for the rain to pass.

After getting those first few documents in order the week we arrived, the next step was to submit our paperwork to the US Embassy. Well, they only accept paperwork on certain days. Evidently, our courier didn't make it with the paperwork in time for the first available drop-off. Meaning, we waited for an entire week to go by just to get to the next allowed day we could submit our paperwork. Needless to say, we all went with the courier to ensure that our paperwork got submitted.

By the next week- our third week in Africa, other families were getting appointments at the embassy for the end of the week. In fact, everyone got an appointment, except us. Insert sad face emoji.

Remember we'd prayed for God to do something so big in our adoption that when people heard our story, they'd have to believe in Him? Welp, by Wednesday, we prayed about it and decided we were going to go on faith and book tickets. Adoption Airfare got things set-up for us. And we sent a pleading email to the embassy. It went something like this:

- To whom it may concern: My husband and I have been in Africa for nearly 3 weeks. My husband's leave from working expires this Friday. We've been praying since we got our son's referral that we'd have him home by his first birthday. That's this Saturday. Our paperwork was submitted Monday. If there's any possibility that we could receive an appointment this week, we'd sincerely appreciate it. If not, we understand. Thank you for your consideration.

We woke up the next morning with no email in our inbox. No response from the Embassy.

And I know this is strange to say, but we had peace. Were we discouraged about the lack of email? Yeah, of course we were. But we had confidence in Christ. We believed we'd been obedient and had faith to reach out to the Embassy and pursue airline tickets. So, while there was discouragement, we had peace knowing we'd been faithful. Take heart. You can have peace in the midst of discouragement.

Then, at breakfast, our agent came and said we had an appointment!!! To pack our things, we were going to the Embassy on Friday. Would you believe that out of all the families, we were seen first at the Embassy? Of course, you can believe it. At this point, if nothing else, I hope I've convinced you that God is good and does crazy awesome things. Things that are even bigger and better than we could ask for or imagine!

Then. We went home. We had 3 flights.

- Addis to Dubai. 4hrs.
- Dubai to Washington, DC. 14 hrs.
- Washington, DC to Charlotte. 1 hr.

And it was on the 14 hours stretch that I began throwing up and other things. Yep, turns out what our son had was contagious. At least- we think we got it from him. That was such a fun flight. Not. The flight attendants on Emirates were amazing though. A few hours in, they came out singing happy birthday to our son. They gave him a cupcake birthday platter and took his picture. And, as soon as they walked away, I promptly threw-up all over his nice cupcake.

Y'all, God even ordained the sweet little man that sat beside us. He didn't say a word about me throwing up and having to constantly get up and go to the bathroom that entire flight. He just let me pass by. At one point, he even went and sat in a flight-attendant's seat. Poor guy. Sweet guy. Chase walked around with our son for most of the flight, to avoid my sickness and to keep him entertained. The flight attendants, again, were wonderful and took pictures of them both and gave us a frame.

Fun fact. Turns out that liver failure we went into-yeah, that was called Hepatitis A. Y'all. Get your shots. I don't care how rushed you are to get to your child's court appointment. Go to the health department. Roll up your sleeve. If the shot costs $1,000, get it. Our medical bills were almost an additional ⅓ of our adoption costs all because we missed that one shot. Thankfully, there's such a thing as payment plans. And here's the thing, we didn't intentionally not get the shot. We were just so rushed that it wasn't even on our radar. We completely forgot. So, go ahead now, mark some time out over the next few months and go get those shots. That way it's a done deal!

The flight from Washington, DC to Charlotte was surreal. I'd driven through Charlotte countless times over those past three years. Every time I saw a plane, I said, "That's going to be us one day, bringing our son home." And then, I'd cry, thinking about how awesome it was going to be to be on that plane one day.

And then, on August 29th, 2015, that was us. Bringing our son home. On his 1st birthday.

I shared his story- our story, with everyone in that back corner of the plane. It was crazy. Flying home. Telling them all the many things that'd just happened over the past 3 weeks.

We landed and immediately walked to a waiting area full of signs and loved ones. About 30 people were there to celebrate my son's homecoming! These were the people that had journeyed with us. They'd prayed with us. They'd laughed with us. They'd cried with us. They'd given generously to us to bring our son home. And they were there, when we came home. Oh man, that moment. It was one for the books.

We went from there straight to Chick-fil-A. Because, of course that's the first American food he needs right?!!

And we had his 1-year birthday party at Chick-fil-a with 30 of our closest friends and family. A three-year-long prayer, answered. Our son wouldn't have to celebrate another birthday without us. He wouldn't have to go to bed one more time without mommy or daddy to rock him to sleep and pray with him. He'd forever have mommy and daddy to love him, hold him, hug him, kiss his booboos, and tell him every day of his precious life, that God loves him, adopted him, and brought. him. home.

Our family has continued to love and grow and learn since bringing our son home. There were still several things we needed to do:

- Readopt in NC
- 3 Post Adoption Reports
- File for NC birth certificate
- Apply for social security card
- Annual reports until he's 18

As of January 2018, we have completed all of the steps- until we learn there's more. That's something we've learned, too. Things are always changing. And that's something you just gotta roll with.

So, our journey officially began in March of 2013 and we received his NC birth certificate in January of 2018. 5 years. Was it worth it? He sure was.

OTHER RELEVANT BOOKS

Christian Publishing House

ISBN-13: 978-1-945757-91-4

ISBN-10: 1-945757-91-4

Heather Freeman &
Edward D. Andrews

THIRTEEN
REASONS WHY
YOU SHOULD
KEEP LIVING

When Hope and
Love Vanish?

Christian Publishing House

ISBN-13: 978-1-945757-47-1

ISBN-10: 1-945757-47-7

THE OUTSIDER

Coming-of-Age In
This Moment

EDWARD D. ANDREWS &
JEFFREY JORDAN

Christian Publishing House

ISBN-13: 978-1-945757-60-0

ISBN-10: 1-945757-60-4

For I delight in the law of God, in my inner being, but I see in my members another law waging war against the law of my mind and making me captive to the law of sin that dwells in my members.—The Apostle Paul (Rom. 7:22-23)

WAGING WAR

A Christian's Cognitive Behavioral Therapy Workbook

Heather Freeman

Christian Publishing House

ISBN-13: 978-1-945757-42-6

ISBN-10: 1-945757-42-6

GOD WILL GET YOU
THROUGH THIS
Hope and Help for
Your Difficult Times

EDWARD D. ANDREWS

Christian Publishing House

ISBN-13: 978-1-945757-72-3

ISBN-10: 1-945757-72-8

FEARLESS

Be Courageous and Strong Through
Your Faith In These Last Days

EDWARD D. ANDREWS

Christian Publishing House
ISBN-13: 978-1-945757-69-3

ISBN-10: 1-945757-69-8

Kelley Lambert

Christian Publishing House
ISBN-13: 978-1-945757-74-7

ISBN-10: 1-945757-74-4

Bible Principles

TURN OLD HABITS INTO NEW HABITS

Why and How the Bible Makes a Difference

EDWARD D. ANDREWS

Christian Publishing House
ISBN-13: 978-1-945757-73-0

ISBN-10: 1-945757-73-6

Kelley Lambert

Christian Publishing House
ISBN-13: 978-1-945757-86-0
ISBN-10: 1-945757-86-8

Author of Over 75 Books

PROMISES OF GOD'S GUIDANCE

God Show Me Your Ways, Teach Me Your
Paths, Guide Me In Your Truth and Teach Me

EDWARD D. ANDREWS

Christian Publishing House
ISBN-13: 978-1-945757-87-7

ISBN-10: 1-945757-87-6

Author of Over 75 Books

BLESSED BY GOD IN SATAN'S WORLD

How All Things Are
Working for Your Good

EDWARD D. ANDREWS

Christian Publishing House
ISBN-13: 978-1-945757-88-4

ISBN-10: 1-945757-88-4

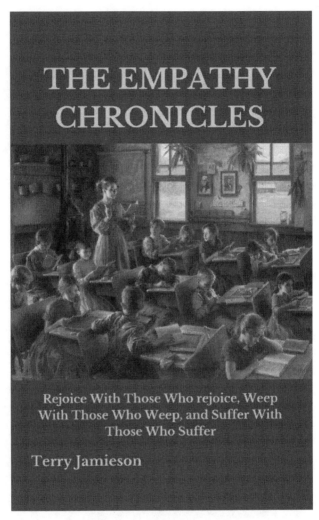

THE EMPATHY
CHRONICLES

Rejoice With Those Who rejoice, Weep
With Those Who Weep, and Suffer With
Those Who Suffer

Terry Jamieson

Christian Publishing House
ISBN-13: 978-1-945757-35-8
ISBN-10: 1-945757-35-3

Made in the USA
Columbia, SC
24 July 2022

63956335R00078